ADHD
Deceptive Diagnosis

By
David M. Tyler, Ph.D.
& Kurt P. Grady, Pharm. D.

ADHD
Deceptive Diagnosis
by David M. Tyler, Ph.D.
& Kurt P. Grady, Pharm.D.

Scripture references are quoted from
The New American Standard Version of the Bible
and where noted,
The King James Version
and The New King James Version

Cover design by Melanie Schmidt

ISBN 1-885904-70-3

PRINTED IN THE UNITED STATES OF AMERICA
BY
FOCUS PUBLISHING

Table of Contents

Introduction

This is not a book on child psychology. It is not just another pragmatic approach to parenting a child labeled ADHD. The authors are not proposing a new method. Instead, our goal is to present the principles of biblical parenting as they pertain to the behaviors associated with the label ADHD. We have attempted to do this with as much clarity as possible. We are convinced that if Christian parents understand and apply the simple principles set forth in Scripture they can rear their children in a way that honors Christ. It is our desire to make parents aware of two things: first, what the Bible has to say about these behaviors, and, second, how to help their children change.

Children Are Blessed Gifts

God's design is that all children, even those labeled with ADHD, are blessed gifts. Children should not be seen as a burden, but a benediction from God to grace our lives with fulfillment, meaning, and happiness. Parenthood is God's gift to us.

Even in a fallen world contaminated by sin, children are living proof of God's love and mercy. Adam and Eve's rebellion toward God occurred before they conceived any children. Nevertheless, God preserved them and permitted Adam and Eve to fulfill the command given before the fall; "Be fruitful and multiply" (Genesis 1:28). In these words God would set in motion a plan of redemption embracing "a great multitude which no one could count, from every nation and all tribes and peoples and tongues" (Revelation 7:9). Adam and Eve's children embodied the hope that fallen sinners could be redeemed.

Adam and Eve recognized children as God's blessing to them. When Cain was born Eve said, "I have gotten a man from the Lord" (Genesis 4:1 KJV). Once again Eve bore a son and said, "For God hath appointed me another seed" (Genesis 4:25). Even the children of unbelievers are tokens of God's blessings. "As for Ishmael... I will bless him." How will God bless Ishmael? God will "make him fruitful and multiply him exceedingly" (Genesis 17:20).

God has given parents the duty of raising their children in the nurture and admonition of the Lord. They are not given the prerogative of delegating that duty to school teachers, peers, or child-care workers. Parents must involve themselves in their children's lives. Parenting is time consuming (Deuteronomy 6:6-7). It is not an easy assignment. The difficulty comes when parents fail to follow the simple principles set forth by God. In neglecting their God-given duty they forfeit the blessing inherent in parenting. Parenting then becomes a burden God never meant for them to bear.

Training up children in the nurture and admonition of the Lord does not always guarantee our parenting will succeed. But isn't Proverbs 22:6 ("Train up a child in the way that he should go, and when he is old he will not depart from it") a promise? Does it promise that if parents train their child in the Lord the child will remain faithful? The answer is no, it is not a promise. Verse 4 says, "The reward of humility and the fear of the Lord are riches, honor and life." However, Proverbs 22:6 is not a guarantee either. Everyone who is humble and fears God does not become rich. Some are poor. They may be persecuted and not honored.

We have all heard stories about children reared in godly homes that later abandoned their faith and grieved their parents. On the other hand, we have heard about godly children whose parents are ungodly and neglectful. Statistically speaking, children influenced by godly parents are more likely to remain faithful than children who grow up in homes where Christ is not honored. The book of Proverbs contains wise sayings, but the wise sayings are not necessarily absolutes. They are not true in every instance. The true measure of parenting has to do with what the *parent* does and not what the *child* does. The focus of success is the character of the parents. Children are quick to understand and will imitate what they see and hear. An affectionate and conscientious parent is a powerful influence in a child's life. Children are never too young to be an accurate observer of their parent's conduct. By that conduct, a child's character may be purified or contaminated. For example, parents want their child to be truthful at all times. However, if the child hears their mother and father tell lies, the child will learn to tell lies. By their example, parents are however unwittingly, molding their child's minds, habits, and character. To the level that parents have followed God's plan for parenting they have succeeded as parents in the eyes of God.

Children have an intellect and do not merely imitate what they see and hear. They are thinking beings. They examine and judge impressions they get, and confirm or reject them according to how they have been taught. Parents must involve themselves, taking great pains in instructing their children to insure no other influences take precedence. For parents to complain that their son or daughter's failures are the fault of their peers is shifting the blame. The parents are to blame because they allowed others to influence their children more than they have themselves.

Some parents may object, roll their eyes, and insist that it is unrealistic to expect them to have more influence with their children than the child's peer group. However, the reason peer groups have influenced children to the degree they have is that parents have simply abdicated the parental role God has required of them. They have invested less time in teaching their children. Television, movies, music, the internet, video games, and other children have become the main source of their children's spiritual, moral, and ethical instruction.

God has made parenting a full-time responsibility. Some parents talk about spending "quality time" with their children. This means they have set aside a number of hours during the week to spend on parenting. This violates the spirit of Deuteronomy 6:7. It guarantees outside influences will have a great affect in shaping the children's character. God solemnly charged parents: "These words, which I am commanding you today, shall be on your heart. You shall teach them diligently to your sons and shall talk of them when you sit in your house and when you walk by the way and when you lie down and when you rise up" (Deuteronomy 6:6-7).

Parents must recognize the mournful fact their children are depraved. If they fail to recognize this sad reality they will fail in their attempts to educate their children. Children possess selfish spirits. Self is king in their lives. How strongly they resemble their fallen parents! Unless a child is instructed in biblical truth he will become a slave to ungodly passions and desires. Wickedness will reign in his heart. However, God gives children tender and supple hearts that can be molded. Enlightened by God's Word, children can differentiate between right and wrong. A child can learn to be responsible toward God and neighbor.

The Facts Change Everything

Have you ever had this kind of experience? You become angry, upset, or happy about a particular event. Later, you discovered an important fact that changed your perception about the event. For example, let's say you are standing in a crowded hallway following the Sunday morning worship service. You are waiting for your wife who has stopped to talk to a friend. You notice Frank Smith hurriedly making his way through the crowd. He passes you and steps on your foot without acknowledging his rude behavior. Frank dashes out the door, leaving you with a sore foot and hurt feelings. You share the incident with your wife on your way home. Both of you are upset with Frank's thoughtless behavior. Later in the week, Frank calls you at your office. He tells you how sorry he is for stepping on your foot last Sunday morning. However, he goes on to explain how he had not been feeling well that morning. When the service ended, he had become very sick and needed to get outside quickly. Suddenly, your perception of the event changed when you had all of the facts and understood the reason for Frank's behavior.

Imagine for a moment a country that drugs six million children with powerful substances to control behavior. A place where parents are told their children are victims of a "brain disease" that causes them to act inappropriately. A disease that, if not treated immediately, could produce a lifetime of failure, disappointment, and underachievement. Frightened by such prospects, the parents are given the "good news" of a safe and mild drug to alleviate the symptoms inflicting havoc in their child's brain. If a parent refuses to accept the pill, they are encouraged to try it on a trial basis. If the magic pill works and calms the child down, then it proves he had the disease after all.

The view that states man is like an animal, a collection of genes, chemicals and stimulus-response behaviors, laid the groundwork for attention deficit disorder, oppositional defiant disorder, and a host of other "diseases." Years ago the symptoms associated with these "disorders" were viewed much differently. They were viewed for what they truly were. If little Archie was reluctant to engage in tasks that required sustained mental effort, made careless mistakes, or did not do his homework, the problem was lack of self-motivation. If he was fidgety, squirmed in his chair, and wouldn't remain seated he was viewed as lacking self-control. If he interrupted others and didn't wait his turn the root problem was poor self-discipline. When Archie behaved in a defiant way and would not comply with rules and requests he was called disobedient. If he pouted, was resentful, and vindictive he was said to have a bad attitude. Lying, stealing and hitting others were sinful. In other words, Archie was expected to behave responsibly. If he behaved irresponsibly, his teacher, school principal, Mom and Dad would teach him to be responsible.

In America today, with psychology deeply rooted in Western thought, children are no longer considered to be capable of volitional control over their actions, attitudes, or thoughts. Their behaviors are said to be beyond their control, affected by hereditary, so-called biochemical imbalances in the brain, food additives, television, or even infant DPT inoculation. Their lack of self-discipline, self-control and self-motivation, disobedience, and bad attitudes are defined as a disease.

This book will help Christian parents who are floundering in the quagmire of unbiblical and contradictory ideas fed to them concerning ADD/ADHD. While its advocates claim ADHD is a brain disease, its opponents, many of which are world renowned psychologists, psychiatrists and neurologists are denying its very existence. It is not a denial of the behaviors; it is a denial the behaviors are caused by a disease.

The biblical model is more than one more "model" or conceptual system to deal with ADHD. Our goal is to help you see biblical truth you have not seen before. When you do, it will change the way you think about the label ADHD. Instead of humanistic psychology you will see Christian theology…, a Person. In place of "disease" we talk about sinful behavior against that Person. Sufferings are trials that reveal our need for comfort and a Comforter. Instead of defining change in unjustified psychological or medical terms we define change as putting off sinful habits and replacing them with Christ-like habits.

The pressures, difficulties, and at times embarrassment that parents go through with a child labeled ADHD are in many cases overwhelming. It is not unusual for entire households to be thrown into turmoil. Family members become divided against one another. Other children in the family may feel ignored or be neglected. Everyone's life is focused on the one child and the chaos he or she creates. Parents respond with a level of anger they would not have thought possible. They react with accusations and ultimatums. In addition, they may become confused and frustrated because of all the fad theories and sure-cures that have disappointed them. They oftentimes feel at a loss to know how best to help their child.

Prayer is a never-failing remedy and comfort to these parents. Sometimes their only solace is when they are on their knees praying to

God. However, parents need to realize there are times when prayer is not enough. There are even times when praying is not the thing to do. Moses was on his knees praying God would deliver His people. Then the Lord said to Moses, "Why are you crying out to Me?" (Exodus 14:15). God was saying to Moses, Moses this is not the time for prayer. It is the time for taking action. "Tell the sons of Israel to go forward" (Exodus 14:15).

There comes a time when praying parents must take godly action. Do not continue to pray and wait and pray and wait. Do not keep worrying and talking about it. Move forward!

Archie's parents must commit themselves to teach, rebuke, correct, and train Archie in righteousness (2 Timothy 3:16; Deuteronomy 6:5-9; Ephesians 6:4). Changing years of habitual behavior will take patience on their part. Schedules and routines may have to be temporarily changed. Mom and dad cannot be cold, or lukewarm in their effort to help Archie put-off and put-on. They must be boiling with holy enthusiasm. Forward, forward, forward is the motto. Christ-likeness is the goal for themselves and Archie.

This book is about giving hope. It may seem that the easiest thing to do is to give up in despair. As you read on, we are confident that you will find help. The Apostle Paul says, "And we know that God causes all things to work together for good to those who love God, to those who are called according to His purpose" (Romans 8:28). The key words in the verse are "work together." It is hard to discern the picture of a puzzle when only a few pieces are in place. When most or all the pieces are in their proper place the picture is clear. God has a plan for you and your child. Yes, He is at work in your circumstances. However, we usually don't realize immediately the good God is doing. Believers only see a very small part of the puzzle. This is an opportunity for parents to minister to their children and to be part of what God is doing in their life. They must never allow themselves or their child to believe God is distant and uninvolved. The Bible teaches God is near and active in their lives. Every moment is a God moment.

True success cannot be achieved by following human techniques. It will only come from a faithful commitment to the sufficiency of God's Word. You say, "I have tried everything." Perhaps you have not tried what is written in the following pages.

How to Use This Book

Secular books regarding ADHD are quite common. Christian books on rearing children are also readily available. However, to our knowledge, a book by Christian authors who seek to biblically address behaviors in children that lead to an ADHD diagnosis is nonexistent. This book attempts to fill that gap.

Parents today need scripturally relevant practical information that can be put in place immediately. This book can be described as "how and why". Part one (how) is very practical in nature, but lacks depth and background information. However, understanding the "why" behind practical suggestions made by others is equally important and this information is found in part two (why?). In order to provide a truly useful book, we believe both elements are absolutely required. You want to know what to do right now (how), and you need to be assured that what you are doing is absolutely grounded in the Word of God (why).

With that, there are really two ways to use this book. First, you can read it from front to back. Second, you can read through part one and read the section we have referenced in part two before moving to the next section or chapter in part one. You may actually want to do both. Either way (or both!) it is our most genuine desire to equip Christians to deal with the issue of ADHD behaviors in a Biblically faithful manner. We hope you find this book useful in that pursuit.

David M. Tyler
Kurt P. Grady

Chapter 1
ADHD: No Consensus

What do psychiatrists, the "wise" of this age, know?
Their goal is not to bring individuals into conformity
with the way of Christ but rather to help them adjust
to the ways of the world. But Christ told us that the
way of the world and his way are in opposition.
                    Seth Farber, *Unholy Madness:*
                    The Church's Surrender to Psychiatry

For over 19 centuries the Church of Jesus Christ did not
have the "benefit" of clinical psychology to assist them
with parenting. Yet for centuries, Christian parents
were still able to obey God's command to "bring up"
their children "in the discipline and instruction of the
Lord" (Ephesians 6:4).
                    Lou Priolo, *Teach Them Diligently*

Horrific sins, such as talking out of turn, not completing assignments, not paying attention and just about anything that might irritate a parent or teacher is all a child has to be observed doing to be diagnosed as having ADHD. As someone once said, "It seems as if childhood itself has been termed a disease."

What does the Bible say about the behaviors that make up the label ADHD? How can you help little Archie change?

We believe the Holy Scriptures are not only able to make men wise unto salvation (2 Timothy 3:16), but also explain why Archie does not pay attention, is impulsive and hyperactive. We do not believe that ADHD is a disease. We are not saying there is nothing wrong with Archie; we are saying he does not have a disease. However, Biblical counselors are not the only ones who do not believe ADHD is a disease.

Psychologist John K. Rosemond in the Foreword of David B. Stein's book, *Unraveling the ADD/ADHD Fiasco* wrote:

For almost two decades I have witnessed a dark—I'll be so bold as to term it evil—trend in psychology and psychiatry. I have watched, often incredulous, as members of these two respected professions mass-marketed two nonexistent diseases, Attention Deficit Disorder (ADD) and Attention Deficit Hyperactive Disorder (ADHD), to the American public. The success of this propaganda effort has resulted in the victimization of millions of parents and children.[1]

David B. Stein, Ph.D., a practicing clinical psychologist, addressed the issue of psychological testing for children suspected to have ADHD in his book *Ritalin Is Not the Answer.* Stein wrote (page 25):

No psychological test can indicate an ADD or ADHD disease. These tests are merely checklists, rating scales, or observations of a child's attention during the test administration. ...These tests are only structured guidelines for observing behavior. They do not measure abnormalities in the body or brain. When a psychologist says your child tested positive for ADD or ADHD, we poor parents are deluded into a misperception that this is a disease. Do not confuse a psychologist's label with a disease. The tests only confirm the labels. They do not indicate or detect any disease entity.[2]

Thomas Armstrong, Ph.D. and former special education teacher, in the Preface of his book *The Myth of the ADD Child* wrote:

Through an aggressive public relations campaign, solid support from the medical community, and scores of well-meaning books and tapes for parents on helping "the ADD child," millions of parents and teachers have been enchanted into believing in the existence of a discrete psychiatric illness called 'attention deficit disorder' that supposedly afflicts millions of American children[3]

There is no cure for ADD, because there is no such thing as ADD.[4]

---

[1] David B. Stein, Ph.D., *Unraveling the ADD/ADHD Fiasco*, (Kansas City, MO: Andrews McMeel, 2001), p. ix.

[2] David B. Stein, Ph.D., *Ritalin Is Not the Answer*, (San Francisco, CA: Jossey-Bass Publishers, 1999), p. 25.

[3] Thomas Armstrong, Ph.D., *The Myth of the A.D.D. Child*, (New York, N.Y: 1995), Preface.

[4] *Ibid.*, p. 58.

Lawrence H. Diller M.D. in his book *Running on Ritalin* wrote:

> Looking back over the history of the syndrome, none of the proposed causes—from brain damage to unspecified nervous system dysfunction to dysfunctional families—had ever been confirmed by research.[5]

Russell Barkley, Ph.D., psychologist and a key advocate for the disease model of ADHD, wrote in his book *Taking Charge of ADHD: The Complete Authoritative Guide for Parents* (page 22):

> There are no lab tests or measures that are of value in making a diagnosis of ADHD, so blood work, urinalysis, chromosome studies, EEGs, average evoked responses, MRIs, and computed tomography (CT scans) should not be used routinely in the evaluation of ADHD children.[6]

Peter R. Breggin, M.D. and psychiatrist in his book *Talking Back to Ritalin* speaks to measuring the level of activity in the brain and how it does not demonstrate abnormality:

> The basic aim of the SPECT (single photon emission computed tomography) and PET (positron emission tomography) studies is to find areas of the brain that are comparatively hypoactive or hyperactive in children or adults diagnosed with ADHD addresses nothing more than relative level of brain function. It's roughly equivalent to taking the normal variations in temperature of various parts of the body. If you happen to be using particular muscles, for example, their energy utilization will go up compared to other muscles that have not been active. The active muscles may even feel warm to the touch. These rough measures of energy in no way indicate an abnormality... They only indicate that these muscles were recently exercised more than the colder muscles. Similarly, if you are visually active at a given moment, the visual cortex of your brain may consume relatively more glucose during that

---

[5] Lawrence H. Diller, M.D., *Running On Ritalin*, (New York, N.Y: Bantam Books, 1998), p. 54.

[6] Russell Barkley, Ph.D., *Taking Charge of ADHD: The Complete Authoritative Guide for Parents*, (New York, N.Y: The Guilford Press, 2000), p. 22.

time. These relative degrees of activity say nothing about whether the activity is abnormal or normal. In fact, these differences can and do occur from moment to moment all day long in perfectly normal brains... Pictures of multi-colored brain scans in newsmagazines and presentations can be an especially seductive touch. The use of different colors to highlight degrees of intensity adds an aura of science to brain scan maps, and makes them look much more complex than they are.[7]

Breggin calls this the "brain scan scam."

If these people do not believe ADHD is a disease, then what do they believe the behaviors represent? Peter R. Breggin wrote in his book *Toxic Psychiatry*:

...Failure to comply with requests and prohibitions. The central problem is obedience.[8]

Lawrence Diller, M.D. and psychiatrist in his book *Running on Ritalin* said:

It's not a chemical imbalance—it is a living imbalance.[9]

While these men, and others, are on the right track by insisting better structure, discipline, parenting, schooling and personal responsibility, they ultimately go wrong and fall short because they do not look to Scripture. Man's fundamental problems have to do with sin, salvation, and sanctification, whatever form those problems take. The Bible says "For the Lord gives wisdom; From His mouth come knowledge and understanding" (Proverbs 2:6). It is not only true the Lord gives us understanding with regard to how to be saved, He also shows us the causes and cures of depression, anxiety, fear, and even the behaviors labeled ADHD.

What ADHD is and what causes it is anybody's guess and that is exactly what it is –anybody's guess. Some of the "experts" say ADHD is caused by a chemical imbalance. Others insist it is related to diet (food additives, artificial flavors, sugar, etc.), while others insist it has a genetic cause. Some, in spite of the fact there is no known cause or pathology, are convinced it is a disease. Others say it is not a disease. Still others believe the behaviors are related to environment (poor

---

[7] Peter R. Breggin, *Talking Back to Ritalin*, (Cambridge, MA: Perseus Publishing, 2001), p. 174.

[8] Peter R. Breggin, *Toxic Psychiatry*, (New York, N.Y: St. Martin's Press, 1991), p. 280.

[9] Lawrence Diller, p. 78.

parenting, teaching, home life, etc.).

If one could sum up, in a word, the state of psychiatry and psychology as it pertains to ADHD, that word would be "confusion." There is no consensus in the medical community on ADHD. There is a consensus among physicians when it comes to heart disease and diabetes. These conditions can be validated by an objective test. This is not true of ADHD as well as other so-called "diseases of the mind." How would you feel if there was no consensus among dentists on how to do dentistry, among engineers on how to build bridges, or among air traffic controllers on how to direct aircraft? How comfortable would you feel boarding an airplane in Saint Louis knowing that the rules and procedures for managing air traffic are different along your way to Boston? How confident would you feel taking your children to a doctor to be treated for a condition and allowing them to be placed on a medication similar to cocaine, when there is no consensus among doctors as to the cause, treatment, or even whether the condition is a real disease?

When the National Institute of Health held a special conference concerning the diagnosis and treatment of ADHD in 1998, they issued a summary statement of their findings. They concluded there is no independent, valid test to diagnose ADHD. This means there is no objective measurement for diagnosing ADHD. You cannot draw blood and find it. You can not perform a CT scan and see it. There is nothing you can objectively find to prove a diagnosis of ADHD. Nothing has changed. There is still no proof of disease.

The Diagnostic and Statistical Manual of Mental Disorders, Fourth Edition, Text Revision states, "There are no laboratory tests, neurological assessments, or attentional assessments that have been established as diagnostic in the clinical assessment of Attention-Deficit/Hyperactive Disorder."[10] Nevertheless, proponents insist, that although the technology is not available to make an objective diagnosis today, proof is coming in the near future.

Using the same argument, Doctor Grady and I can invent a childhood disease today and call it Tyler-Grady Disease. We could start diagnosing it, and have prescriptions written to medicate people who "have it." Although no laboratory tests have been established to diagnose Tyler-Grady Disease we tell the public we will validate it in the future. No big deal! Will you allow us to medicate your child?

---

[10] American Psychiatric Association, *Diagnostic and Statistical Manual of Mental Disorders, Fourth edition Text Revision*. (Washington DC: American Psychiatric Association, 2000), pp. 88,89.

Questions Christian Parents Need to Ask Their Physician about ADHD

1) Why do psychiatrists, psychologists and doctors disagree as to whether ADHD even exists?

2) Why is there such widespread disagreement, among psychiatrists, psychologists and doctors who believe it exists, as to what constitutes ADHD?

3) What medical, laboratory tests (blood, urine, bodily fluids, etc) were performed on my child to scientifically prove your diagnosis of ADHD? Without following standard medical procedures are you not basing your conclusions simply on behavior?

4) What are the immediate and long-term side-effects of the medication you want to prescribe?

Myths about ADHD

1) *Myth*. Brain / PET scans can determine your child has ADHD. *Truth*. There is no brain / PET scan that can determine a child has ADHD.

2) *Myth*. ADHD is a disease like cancer or diabetes. *Truth*. ADHD is not a disease.

   i. Cancer and diabetes can be objectively diagnosed (biopsies, blood, etc.). Certain treatments and therapies (chemotherapy) can be given and a doctor can clearly observe as to whether the cancer is shrinking, inactive or growing. Diabetes is treated using insulin or oral medications. Objective blood glucose measurements are used to monitor control of diabetes.

   ii. You would not treat a person with chemotherapy unless it was determined, using objective tests, they had cancer. In the same way, why would you administer a DEA Schedule 2 drug (same classification as Cocaine, Morphine, and Methamphetamine) without proof your child's ADHD even exists?

3) *Myth*. If the medication works and improves your child's behavior, it proves your child really had ADHD. *Truth*. Stimulant drugs (like Ritalin™) have the same effect on "normal" children or adults.

Chapter 2
The Biblical Diagnosis

One reason why many Christians fail to change is because they try to change by breaking bad habits. True change will not take place if you only concentrate on breaking a bad habit. A key biblical principle for change is this: We don't break bad habits, we replace them.

Armand P. Tiffe, *Transformed Into His Likeness*

In reference to your former manner of life, you lay aside the old self, which is being corrupted in accordance with the lusts of deceit, and that you be renewed in the spirit of your mind and put on the new self, which in the likeness of God has been created in righteousness and holiness of the truth.

Apostle Paul, *Ephesians 4:22-24*

The Diagnostic and Statistical Manual of Mental Health Disorders (Fourth Edition, text revision) is a serious looking text with nearly 1000 pages in the current paperback edition. The primary stated benefit of the DSM is to capture in one volume a common set of definitions useful in diagnosing and categorizing mental illnesses. Psychiatrists, psychologists, counselors, social workers, etc., use the DSM daily for diagnostic and billing guidance. The DSM has become the central element in the diagnosing ADHD.

The DSM-IV-TR Criteria for ADHD

ADHD is divided into three categories or types. 1) ADHD, *Combined Type*: if both criterion 1A and 1B are met for the past 6 months, 2) ADHD, *Predominantly Inattentive Type*: if criterion 1A is met but criterion 1B is not met for the past six months 3) ADHD, *Predominantly Hyperactive-Impulsive Type*: if Criterion 1B is met but Criterion 1A is not met for the past six months.

A. Either (1) or (2):

    (1) Six (or more) of the following symptoms of **inattention** have persisted for at least 6 months to a degree that is maladaptive and inconsistent with developmental level:

<u>Inattention</u>

        a. often fails to give close attention to details or makes careless mistakes in schoolwork, work, or other activities

        b. often has difficulty sustaining attention in tasks or play activities

        c. often does not seem to listen when spoken to directly

        d. often does not follow through on instructions and fails to finish schoolwork, chores, or duties in the workplace (not due to oppositional behavior or failure to understand instructions)

        e. often has difficulty organizing tasks and activities.

        f. often avoids, dislikes, or is reluctant to engage in tasks that required sustained mental effort (such as schoolwork or homework)

        g. often loses things necessary for tasks and activities (e.g. toys, school assignments, pencils, books, or tools)

        h. is often easily distracted by extraneous stimuli

        i. is often forgetful in daily activities

    (2) Six (or more) of the following symptoms of **hyperactivity-impulsivity** have persisted for at least 6 months to a degree that is maladaptive and inconsistent with developmental level:

<u>Hyperactivity</u>

        a. often fidgets with hands or feet or squirms in seat

        b. often leaves seat in classroom or in other situations in which remaining seated is expected

        c. often runs about or climbs excessively in situations in which it is inappropriate (in adolescents or adults, may be limited to subjective feelings of restlessness)

      d. often has difficulty playing or engaging in leisure activities quietly

      e. is often "on the go" or often acts as if "driven by a motor"

      f. often talks excessively

Impulsivity

      g. often blurts out answers before questions have been completed.

      h. often has difficulty awaiting turn.

      i. often interrupts or intrudes on others (e.g., butts into conversations or games).

B. Some hyperactive-impulsive or inattention symptoms that caused impairment were present before age 7 years.

C. Some impairment from the symptoms is present in two or more settings (e.g. at school [work] and at home).

D. There must be clear evidence of clinically significant impairment in social, academic, or occupational functioning.

E. The symptoms do not occur exclusively during the course of a Pervasive Developmental Disorder, Schizophrenia, or other Psychotic Disorder and are not better accounted for by another mental disorder (e.g. Mood Disorder, Anxiety Disorder, Dissociative Disorder, or a Personality Disorder).[11]

These diagnostic terms are also ever-present in normal children. Children are active. If your six year old was sitting quietly on the sofa for a period of time you would be concerned. You would probably ask him or her, "Are you okay? Do you feel alright?" Edward Hallowell and John Ratey in their book *Driven to Distraction* wrote: "The hallmark symptoms of ADHD – distractibility, impulsivity, and high activity – are so commonly associated with children in general that the diagnosis is often not considered... How can you tell a spoiled child from an ADD child?"[12]

---

[11] American Psychiatric Association: *Diagnostic and Statistical Manual of Mental Disorders, Fourth Edition, Text Revision.* (Washington, DC, American Psychiatric Association, 2000). pp. 92,93.

[12] Edward Hallowell and John Ratey, *Driven to Distraction*, (New York, NY: Simon & Schuster, 1994), p. 41.

Few people would argue that, under certain conditions, all children exhibit the behaviors of inattention, hyperactivity and impulsivity. The question is whether or not the symptoms represent disease. The symptoms are so vague and there are no laboratory tests to diagnose the condition.

Notice, six symptoms over a period of six months qualifies for a diagnosis. Dr. Peter Breggin wrote, "Six items from either list qualify a child for the diagnosis. There is no scientific validity or clinical reality to this particular number."[13]

In all the behaviors listed in the DSM-IV-TR the word "*often*" is used to describe the problem behavior. The child *often* does not give close attention to details, *often* fidgets with his hands or feet, or often blurts out answers. One boy diagnosed with ADHD was said to play with his pencil a lot. How does the word "often" apply to him? Does it mean he plays with his pencil three times in an hour? Is it the frequency that he plays with his pencil that makes it a symptom of ADHD? Does he play with his pencil every day, every other day, in the mornings, afternoons; how is "often" defined? What exactly is he doing with his pencil? Is he tapping it on his desk, chewing on it, rolling it between his fingers? Could these behaviors indicate something else? Could it suggest boredom? Is he anxious about something going on in his family life? What if a child only demonstrates four of these behaviors instead of the six required for a diagnosis? Does this indicate he has a mild case of ADHD? Is it like a person who has a pre-cancerous condition? Does he have a pre-ADHD or a near ADHD condition? The DSM-IV-TR says there are times when a child is doing something he likes to do when he doesn't exhibit signs of the "disease."

> Symptoms typically worsen in **situations** that require sustained attention or mental effort or lack intrinsic appeal or novelty (listening to classroom teachers, doing class assignments, listening to or reading lengthy materials, or working on monotonous, repetitive tasks). Signs of the disorder may be minimal or absent when the person is under very strict control, is in a novel setting, is engaged in especially interesting activities...[14]

---

[13] Peter R. Breggin, M.D., *Talking Back to Ritalin*, (Cambridge, MA: Perseus Publishing, 2001), p. 152.

[14] American Psychiatric Association, *Diagnostic and Statistical Manual of Mental Disorders Fourth Edition Text Revision*, (Washington, DC: 2000), pp.86,87 (bold ours).

Perhaps the *situation* the child is in has more to do with it than an unsubstantiated disease.

Biblical counselors and parents must take the ADHD label and demystify it by using biblical language. For example, the word "often" is repeatedly used in the DSM-IV-TR to describe the symptoms of ADHD. Everyone recognizes the ADHD individual is characterized by repetitive behavior. For example, *often* fails to pay close attention, *often* does not seem to listen, and *often* loses things and so on. The psychiatrist and psychologist attribute the repetitive behavior to disease, the biblical counselor to habit[15] (The biblical doctrine of habit is discussed in greater detail in chapter 11, *The Process of Biblical Change*).

The aim of biblical counseling is the sanctification of the believer. There is an intimate relation between sanctification and counseling the child labeled ADHD. Counseling is an integral part of the sanctification process for someone struggling in a particular area. For counseling to be truly Christian in nature it must be carried out in harmony with the regeneration and sanctifying work of the Holy Spirit. The character qualities held forth to parents and their child, such as love, joy, peace, patience, kindness, goodness, faithfulness, gentleness and self-control is what the Bible calls "fruit," or the workings of the Holy Spirit. It is useless to generate these qualities apart from Him. Nevertheless, some non-Christian and even Christian counselors attempt to do just that. Such an approach is rebellion against God. It is a denial of Scripture and is based on the humanistic presuppositions of man's autonomy and innate goodness.[16]

There are times, when in order to effect change that pleases God, one believer needs the aid of another believer. Parents who are unfamiliar with what the Bible teaches about the behaviors labeled ADHD need someone trained in biblical counseling. It may be your pastor, a friend or someone who counsels biblically in a formal sense. Through the ministry of God's Word and the power of the Holy Spirit,

---

[15] It should be understood that biblical counseling is not a Bible-based form of Skinnerian behaviorism. The God-given ability for man to formulate habits, while learned and observed by Skinner and other behaviorists, does not mean a biblical counselor is a behaviorist. Biblical counselors are not behaviorists from a biblical perspective. It should also be understood that when biblical counselors discuss behavior they are including both mental and emotional patterns.

[16] See Jay E. Adam's book *Competent to Counsel* for a more extensive explanation on this subject.

substantial change is brought about in the Christian's life. It is a God-ward change toward the likeness of Jesus Christ.[17] It glorifies God. There are times when sanctification is stymied and can only proceed by effective biblical counseling. Paul wrote:

> **Brethren, even if a man is caught in any trespass, you who are spiritual, restore such a one in a spirit of gentleness; each one looking to yourself, lest you too be tempted. Bear one another's burdens, and thus fulfill the law of Christ** (Galatians 6:1-2, italics ours).

Every Christian must realize, whether they have been called into full-time counseling ministry or not, they will counsel someone at some time. Parents counsel their children. A husband counsels his wife and a wife her husband. Church members teach, admonish, and encourage one another (Colossians 3:16, Romans 15:14). Life is full of hardships, difficulties and problems. Christians too, experience anger, fear, depression, anxiety, inattention and lack of self-control. They need someone to come alongside them to instruct and encourage them. The obligation of every believer to counsel, formally or informally, cannot be ignored. When one believer discovers another believer who is caught, bound, and mastered by a sin from which he cannot extricate himself, he is duty-bound to help. To "restore" him from the burden of a particular sin is the job of the biblical counselor. The moving forward of sanctification in the Christian's life is the goal of counseling.

The child's progressive change toward Christ-likeness, sanctification, is the work of the Holy Spirit through God's Word. Jesus joined sanctification and truth together when he said, "Sanctify them in the truth; Thy word is truth" (John 17:17). Psychological theories and therapies will never produce Godliness and Christ-likeness. God's truth leads to holiness. Man's error, directly or indirectly, leads to sin. Twisted doctrine will ultimately lead to a twisted life. Sadly, God's people are being led astray by other believers, who attempt to integrate the theories of men with God's sufficient Word. The Apostle John wrote:

> **Watch yourselves that you might not lose what we have accomplished, but that you may receive a full reward. Anyone who goes too far and does not abide**

---

[17] There is no such thing as change that is neutral. A person is either moving toward or away from God.

in the teaching of Christ, does not have God; the one who abides in the teaching, he has both the Father and the Son (2 John 1:8-9, italics ours).

Going beyond what Christ taught means they add to Christ's words which prove they do not abide in His teaching. You must not add to Christ's words. They are the words that sanctify. His words are fixed. A counselor may study and gain better understanding of the original text, but the text which he has is "perfect, restoring the soul" (Psalm 19:7).

A change in behavior (sanctification) is one of the discernible evidences of the Spirit's presence and work in a believer's life. Maturing Christians, children or adults, seek to deal with their sin by putting it off and putting on righteousness. While they advance in their faith they are never satisfied with their progress. The more they put away sin, the more they notice sinful habits and inclinations that need to be put away. The believer's goal is to please God by putting off the stubborn remnants of sin, and the problems, discomforting feelings of depression, guilt and anxiety that they produce. Paul wrote:

"Knowing this, that our old self was crucified with Him, that our body of sin might be done away with, that we should no longer be *slaves* to sin" (Romans 6:6, italics ours).

The victory over inattention, hyperactivity and impulsivity begins with knowledge. The word "knowing" Paul uses in the above passage, teaches believers that sound knowledge is important to living a life pleasing to God. Maturing faith or Christ-likeness is grounded on biblical principles that must be known before they can work in a child's life.

Paul had previously spoken of the believer's position in Christ (Romans 6:1-5). Now he is referring to the believer's practice or behavior. He mentions the body for the first time. However, Paul is not saying the body, *per se,* is evil and the source of sin (Gnosticism). Man was created with a body and God called it good (Genesis 3:31). Sinful behavior is an expression of the heart manifested by the body. The body is the vehicle of the heart. The heart drives behavior, not the body (Matthew 12:34; 15:19; Proverbs 4:23). Sins such as inattention, hyperactivity and impulsivity are heart issues, not body (or brain) issues.

21

The way sin operates in our body, for example, can be compared to sitting down to eat a meal. There is nothing intrinsically sinful with eating. God made our bodies and we need to eat. However, the food looks wonderful and is so delicious we take this natural body function and push it beyond where it was intended to go. We overeat. We stuff ourselves. The overindulgence is sin, and it can lead to even greater sin if it becomes a *pattern* or *habit* in our life. Habitual overeating can have detrimental effects on the body (weight gain, high blood pressure, high cholesterol, etc.). Self-indulgence can lead to ungratefulness, failure to think of others and give thanks to God, and even complaining if for some reason we are unable at some future point to indulge ourselves as freely.

The formation of sinful habits begins at an early age (2 years old or earlier). When a person is converted, these habits generally do not automatically disappear. They often carry over into their new life as a child of God. A battle ensues within the believer's heart. It is the flesh (the body habituated to sin) warring against the regenerated spirit.

The putting off of sin is what sanctification is all about. Sin's hold over a Christian's body is not absolute. The believer is a new creature with a new heart: the tyranny of sin has been abolished. The Christian has died to sin (Romans 6:2). The chief characteristic of his or her life is no longer sin. The believer does not have to be a slave to sin as he once was. Nevertheless, sinful habits still persist in every believer even to the extent that there are times when sin appears to dominate the Christian's life completely. Progressive sanctification is the process whereby these sinful habits are put off and replaced by new righteous habits through the renewing of one's mind.

Scripture constantly warns us of the danger of becoming habituated to sin of any kind.

> **Knowing this, that our old self was crucified with Him, in order that our body of sin might be done away with, so that we would no longer be *slaves* to sin** (Romans 6:6, italics ours).

> **Therefore do not let sin *reign* in your mortal body so that you obey its lusts** (Romans 6:12, italics ours).

> **And do not *go on presenting* the members of your body to sin...** (Romans 6:13, italics ours).

> **For sin shall not be *master* over you...** (Romans 6:14, italics ours).

For we also once were foolish ourselves, disobedient, deceived, *enslaved* to various lusts and pleasures... (Titus 3:3, italics ours).

For everyone who partakes only of milk is *accustomed* to the word of righteousness, for he is an infant. But solid food is for the mature, who because of *practice* have their senses *trained* to discern good and evil (Hebrews 5:13-14, italics ours)

Not forsaking our own assembling together, as is the *habit* of some, but encouraging one another; and all the more as you see the day drawing near (Hebrews 10:25, italics ours).

Therefore, since we have so great a cloud of witnesses surrounding us, let us also lay aside every encumbrance and the sin which so easily *entangles* us, and let us run with endurance the race that is set before us...(Hebrews 12:1, italics ours).

Summary: For Counselors and Parents

1) The ADHD label must be demystified and replaced by biblical language. Parents must be taught to think biblically and not psychologically about inattention, hyperactivity and impulsivity.

2) When God created mankind he made him with the capacity to formulate habits. Parents must be taught the biblical doctrine and dynamics of habit.

3) Little Archie, like all children and adults, will habituate himself to speak, act, think and be motivated in ways that are displeasing to God.

4) Psychiatrists and psychologists attribute the repetitive behavior to disease; the biblical counselor to habit.

5) The child's progressive change toward Christ-likeness is the goal. Training the child to develop godly habits is what Christ-likeness is all about.

6) Change is a two-factored process and involves putting off sinful habits and replacing them with godly habits.

Exercise in Understanding the "Put-Off" and "Put-On" Dynamic[18]

The purpose of this exercise is to teach Christian parents how to deal with the habitual sins that characterize ADHD. Remember, it is not enough to confess habitual sin. Sinful patterns must be replaced with righteous habits.

On a piece of paper write answers to the following questions.

1) How do you know we have sinned? Read Hebrews 4:12 and John 16:7-8.

2) Do you have to sin? Read Romans 6:6-7, 14.

3) Describe the characteristics of the "old self." Read Ephesians 4:22.

4) What is the "new self" like? Read Ephesians 4:24

5) What are you to "put-off" and "put-on" according to Ephesians 4:22 and 24?

6) According to the following verses what should you "put-off" or "lay aside?" What should you "put-on?"

   a. Ephesians 4:25

   b. Ephesians 4:26, 27

   c. Ephesians 4:28

   d. Ephesians 4:29

   e. Ephesians 4:31-32

   f. Ephesians 5:11

   g. Ephesians 5:4

   h. Ephesians 5:18

   i. Philippians 4:6

   j. Colossians 3:8, 12, 14

   k. Romans 13:12-14

Write down the specific sins in your life that need to be "put-off." Write down what you are to "put-on" in place of these sins.

---

[18] For further study on putting-off sinful habits and replacing them with godly habits see *The Armory Equipment for Spiritual Warfare, Habit Replacement* by Marshall Asher. Published by Focus Publishing, Bemidji, Minnesota. www.focuspublishing.com

Chapter 3
Training in Righteousness

We must never be half-hearted or uncertain in the fight. If you are doubtful about the warfare in which you are engaged you will fight very badly.

D.M. Lloyd-Jones, *The Christian Soldier*

Be strong in the Lord and in the strength of His might. Put on the full armor of God, so that you will be able to stand firm against the schemes of the devil. For our struggle is not against flesh and blood..."

Apostle Paul, *Ephesians 6:10, 11*

Habits are learned ways of responding to life's problems and people. Habits are comfortable, automatic, and carried out without conscious thought or decision. Archie was not born with the behaviors labeled ADHD; he practiced them until they became a part of him. In the same way righteous habits are acquired through practice. There is no such thing as instant sanctification or godliness. There is no pill or formula for becoming like Christ. Paul wrote to Timothy, "discipline yourself for the purpose of godliness" (1 Timothy 4:7). The secret to godliness is discipline. The counselor and Archie's parents must help Archie learn to discipline himself for the purpose of godliness. (We are using the general name, 'Archie'. These principles could apply to 'Annie' as well.) Discipline means work. It means daily effort. It means self-denial. Jesus said to His disciples, "If anyone wishes to come after Me, let him deny himself, and take up his cross, and follow Me" (Matthew 16:24). Denying himself refers to denying the old desires, ways, or practices. Taking up a cross means death. It means putting to death the old habits of the old man. But that is not enough. Where there is putting off in the Scriptures, there is a corresponding putting on. It means saying no to self every day.

Paul said to Timothy, "All Scripture is inspired by God and profitable for teaching, for reproof, for correction, for *training in righteousness*" (2 Timothy 3:16, italics ours). To teach, rebuke, and correct Archie would have been incomplete. Archie needs to learn how to live in such a way that he does not fall back into his old ways of living. The Scriptures provide everything necessary to train Archie in righteousness. Training in righteousness is absolutely essential. The counselor and parents must work closely and consistently in order to help Archie practice the desired behavior. Most biblical counselors will say that it takes four to six weeks of practice to put off a sinful habit and put on the righteous biblical habit. (For an in-depth discussion on the Biblical doctrine of habit read chapter 11, *The Process of Biblical Change*).

Inattentive Category

The DSM says, "Often fails to give close attention to details or makes careless mistakes..."and "Often has difficulty sustaining attention in tasks and play."

Archie's parents need to learn and teach Archie that details matter to God. God is a God of details. The six days of creation demonstrate God is concerned with details. God could have created everything in a moment; however He created in a systematic and orderly way. On day one He created light, day two the heavens, day three He separated the land from seas, and so on. The precision of the earth's rotation on its axis every twenty-four, not twenty-three or twenty –four and a half, hours allows a weatherman to predict sunrise and sunset to the minute. After Adam and Eve sinned, God put into motion a *plan* of redemption. The Old Testament gives us all the details. The seed of the woman can be traced beginning with Adam and Eve's son, Seth, then generations later Noah, Abraham, Isaac, Jacob, Joseph, then David, Solomon, and so on. Then God sent His Son, in "*the fullness of time*" (Galatians 4:4, italics ours). God is concerned about the smallest and, humanly speaking, most insignificant matters. He notices a single sparrow that falls to the ground and dies (Matthew 10:29). He numbers the hairs on our heads (Matthew 10:30).

Archie needs to understand he is accountable to God for even the smallest matters of living. Archie needs to learn to be attentive. Because "foolishness is bound up in the heart of a child" (Proverbs 22:15), children should never determine what tasks and subjects are important to pay attention to. The Scripture constantly commands believers to pay attention. For example, Peter wrote, "Therefore, *prepare* your minds for action, keep *sober* in spirit, *fix* your hope completely on the grace to be brought to you at the revelation of Jesus Christ" (1 Peter 1:13, italics ours). Prepare your minds, keep sober, fix your hope completely on…Jesus Christ, and, in other words, pay attention. In Matthew twenty-four Jesus uses a variety of illustrations, culminating in the *Parable of the Fig Tree*, admonishing alertness (paying attention) to the signs of His coming. As the fig leaf tells us summer is near, so the signs mentioned, false Christs (v: 5), wars (v 6), famines, earthquakes (v: 7), false prophets (v: 11), will warn of His return.

Solomon cautioned children to pay attention to their father and mother's words when he wrote, "*Hear*, my son, your father's instruction and do not forsake your mother's teachings" (Proverbs 1:8, italics ours). "My son, give *attention* to my wisdom, *incline* your ear to my understanding" (Proverbs 5:1, italics ours). In the *Parable of the Ten Virgins* Jesus talks about the uncertainty of the time of His return and the necessity of being ready for it. The parable leads up to the final injunction to "Be on *alert* then, for you do not know the day or the hour [pay attention]" (Matthew 25:13, italics and brackets ours). Paul said believers should pay attention to glorify God in all things. He wrote, "Whether then, you eat or drink or whatever you do, do all to the glory of God" (1 Corinthians 10:31). The greatest example is the young boy Jesus. Mary and Joseph had left Jerusalem with others who had attended the festival. At the end of a day they realized Jesus was not with the company and must have remained behind in Jerusalem. The following morning they returned to Jerusalem. On the third day "they found Him in the temple, sitting in the midst of the teachers, both *listening* (paying attention) to them and asking them questions (Luke 2:46, italics ours).

Question to Ask

"What is Archie's goal and purpose?" Oftentimes, the reason children may not pay attention and make careless mistakes is that they have wrong goals. Their goal may be…

1) To get done with an assignment before their classmates. To win. To be first.

2) To hurry in order to finish quickly and do what they want to do.

3) To avoid the consequences of not getting done on time.

Archie needs to learn good stewardship which includes his thought life (i.e. paying attention), and doing his very best. Being first, hurrying to get done so he can do what he wants are selfish and sinful goals.

Putting-Off and Putting-On

Luke 2:46 is the put on verse to be assigned to Archie to memorize. The put off "not listening" is implied in the verse. Archie needs to put off the sinful habit of not paying attention and replace it with the righteous habit of paying attention. Make seven or eight copies of the put-off and put-on verse. Make the font large enough so it can be read from a distance. Post the put-off and put-on verse in various places around the house. Quiz Archie in the morning and evening on his put-off and put-on verse.

Practicing the Put-On (Righteousness)

These exercises will help Archie practice paying attention to details and avoid careless mistakes. Archie should be praised when he is obedient and does well. He should be reminded his efforts are pleasing to God.

Homework – A

1) PRAYER -- Homework always begins with prayer. Ask God to help Archie in his effort to change. Lead Archie to pray, "Heavenly Father, help me as I practice my put on. Help me to learn to pay attention. Bless my obedience to You and change my heart."

2) REPENTANCE -- Change always begins with repentance and the seeking of forgiveness from God and neighbor (parents, teacher, etc.). There are at least two ways Archie can ask his teacher for forgiveness. One is when other children are not present Archie can ask his teacher for forgiveness for not paying attention. Archie, not the parent, must ask the teacher for forgiveness. Second, Archie can write a letter, buy a card, or create a card on the computer and give it to his teacher that asks for forgiveness.

Homework – B

1) Teach Archie by your example. Do you pay attention when Archie and others speak to you?

Homework – C

1) Read 1 Corinthians 10:31. "Whether, then, you eat or drink or whatever you do, do all for the glory of God." Point out to Archie "whatever" he does he must do to glorify God. This means eating, drinking, playing video games, speaking words, or paying attention. Put all things in a biblical context. He pays attention not primarily to please Mom, Dad and his teacher. He pays attention because God commands him to pay attention and honor those in authority. Pleasing God is the goal.

Homework – D

1) Have Archie bring to the next counseling session what he believes to be his best papers from several of his classes (2 or 3 papers from each class). Using 1 Corinthians 10:31 ("Whether, then, you eat or drink or whatever you do, do all to the glory of God.") evaluate the papers. Look at the details (sentence structure, spelling, legibility, and general neatness, etc.). Ask him, "Did you do your best? Could you have done better? How could you have done better?"

2) From these papers make a list of problems that reoccurred. Using that checklist ask Archie to evaluate future assignments before he hands them in to his teacher.

Homework – E

1) Have Archie's parents review his school homework assignments. Instruct Archie to complete five of the twenty-five math problems assigned in ten minutes. Set a timer. This will give Archie two minutes for each problem. Setting the timer will help get a feeling of success.

2) Within a defined timeframe have Archie construct something. The purpose is to have Archie focus and concentrate on a task that must be completed within a certain amount of time. Many children enjoy hands-on activities. A young child can use square building blocks. An older child can use Legos™, Lincoln Logs™ or modeling clay. Archie must complete the project and tell you what he built.

3) Have Archie and a parent take a walk through the neighborhood, park, field, downtown area or whatever is convenient to their home. Give Archie an assignment before you go. For example, pick something that Archie is interested in, like animals or cars.

Tell Archie on this walk he will have to find five cars and tell you the make and model of each. Or find five dogs, and tell the breed and color of each. For a smaller child their assignment may be to find five different rocks or leaves.

The DSM says, "Often does not seem to listen when spoken to directly."

Archie's parents need to teach him to listen when someone speaks to him. His Mom and Dad listen when Archie speaks to them. His school teacher listens when Archie speaks to him or her. God listens when Archie says his prayers. Archie needs to *learn* to listen. Failure to listen is selfishness and failure to give honor to a parent, teacher, or someone else who is speaking.

A child may ignore an adult if he is doing something he likes or is asked to do something he may not want to do. Selfishly deciding he is not going to listen is sinful. The Bible says, "Honor your father and mother, as the Lord your God has commanded you" (Deuteronomy 5:16), and "Be devoted to one another in brotherly love; give preference to one another in honor" (Romans 12:10). Solomon cautioned children to listen attentively to their father and mother's words when he wrote, "*Hear*, my son, your father's instruction and do not forsake your mother's teachings" (Proverbs 1:8, italics ours). "My son, give *attention* to my wisdom, *incline your ear* to my understanding" (Proverbs 5:1, italics ours). Abraham (the elder) showed honor toward his nephew Lot by allowing him first choice of the land. To honor a person is to show respect for the person. It is to behave in a courteous manner and listen. It is to esteem someone above self (Phil. 2:3). It is selflessness.

It is important for the parents to be resolved to teach Archie what God says about listening and learning. If Archie does not learn to listen to his parents he will not listen to others in authority. He will not listen to the Authority of God's Word. Archie will grow in wisdom as he learns submission and listens to wise counsel from parents, teachers and God (Proverbs 19:20, 27).

Question to Ask:

"What is Archie's goal and purpose?" Archie's goal may be...

1) To do what he wants and not be bothered.

2) Not to have to do what his parents or teachers want him to do. Archie needs to learn that ignoring those in authority is rebellion and displeases God.

3) To ignore authority because he doesn't want to do what others want him to do. For example, his mother wants him to clean his room or come to supper.

Putting-Off and Putting-On

As above Luke 2:46 would be an appropriate put-off and put-on. Another possibility could be Proverbs 1:8 "*Hear,* my son, your father's instruction and *do not forsake your mother's teachings*" (Proverbs 1:8, italics ours). The put-off is Archie forsaking his mother's teaching. The word "mother" would include anyone in authority over him (school teacher, Sunday school teacher, etc.). The put-on on is hearing, and practicing instruction. Make seven or eight copies of the put-off and put-on verse. Make the font large enough so it can be read from a distance. Post the put-off and put-on verse in various places around the house. Quiz Archie in the morning and evening on his put-off and put-on verse.

Practicing the Put-On (Righteousness)

These exercises will help Archie practice paying attention and listening. When giving instructions do not wait for Archie to do what you say. Instead, you say to him, "Get started now." As before, praise Archie when he is obedient and does well. Remind him that his efforts are pleasing to God.

Homework – A

1) Refer to Prayer and Repentance above / Homework A

Homework – B

1) Teach Archie by your example. Do you listen and pay attention when Archie and others speak to you?

Homework – C

1) Help Archie practice paying attention and listening by giving clear visual and verbal instructions. Rather than speaking to Archie from another room the parent should be visible. It is important to have Archie's full attention before talking with him.

2) The parent should touch Archie on his shoulder and call him by name. Give Archie clear and understandable instructions.

3) If a parent is giving more than one instruction he or she should hold up a finger for each instruction. For example, "Archie turn off the computer, hang up your coat, put your boots in the closet and come to supper.

4) Help Archie practice listening by making it a rule he must always verbally respond when spoken to. For example, "OK, Mom, I will turn off the computer." Silence is never acceptable, nor is a grunt of acknowledgement!

The DSM says "often loses things necessary for tasks or activities (i.e. toys, school assignments, pencils, books, or tools)."

Archie lacks organization. He would often lose things. Losing things is not a disease. Orderliness, a Godly characteristic, must be put on. God Himself has a time and place for everything under the sun. "To everything there is a season, and a time to every purpose under the heavens" (Ecclesiastes 3:2).

God created everything in a systematic and orderly fashion. He did not act haphazardly. He ordered every planet to move with mathematical precision in its own orbit. The animal kingdom shows God's orderly ways. What a marvel that at a fixed period of time, creatures in the oceans and on land, migrate great distances. Again, there is order in the way God providentially moves throughout the history of mankind. At first it seems human history is a jumbled series of events. Some have even said the world proves there is no God. However, every event is marching toward a great consummation. The Church of Jesus Christ is orderly. It is like different parts of a body. The eye must never say to the foot "I don't need you." Every member must work according to the gifts of the Holy Spirit.

Everything has its place. The issue with Archie is carelessness and laziness. Paul says God expects us all to be responsible stewards of the things God has given us. He wrote, "It is required of stewards that one be found trustworthy" (1 Corinthians 4:2). Archie's parents need to teach Archie that disorderliness is a sinful habit he must put off.

Questions to Ask:

What is Archie's goal?

1) Is Archie disorderly because he is in a hurry to do something else?

2) Is he disorderly because he likes to be the first to finish?

3) Is he disorderly because he doesn't care how his work looks?

Putting-Off and Putting-On

Archie needs to learn to be better organized in order to please God and neighbor (parents and teachers). A good rule for orderliness is found in 1 Corinthians 14:33, 40. Paul writes, "God is not a God of *confusion*... But all things must be done *properly* and in an *orderly* manner." The put-off is confusion or disorderliness. The put-on is properly and orderly. Make seven or eight copies of the put-off and put-on verse. Make the font large enough so it can be read from a distance. Post the put-off and put-on verse in various places around the house. Quiz Archie in the morning and evening on his put-off and put-on verse.

Practicing the Put-On (Righteousness)

These exercises will help Archie practice being organized. Remember as he practices a behavior he will become habituated to that behavior. Always put Archie's obedience or disobedience in the context of pleasing or displeasing God. Praise Archie when he is obedient and does well.

Homework – A

1) Refer to Prayer and Repentance above / Homework A

Homework – B

1) Teach Archie by example. Show him that everything has its place. Parents set a bad example when they are disorganized. Repent of the sin of not being organized, then get organized. Everything must be in its place. If your house is cluttered have yard sale. Give some things to the Salvation Army. Remember, Mom and Dad need to take the log out of their own eye before they try to take the speck out of Archie's (Matthew 7:1-5).

Homework – C

1) Help Archie make a list of how he is disorderly at home, school and in his personal appearance. Start out simple. Perhaps one item per category. It is inadvisable to overwhelm Archie with a long list.

    a.   Ask Archie if he has ever seen a spider's web? Ask "Have you noticed how perfect the spider makes its web?" Spiders build their houses out of silk that comes from inside their body. Each thread of the spider's web is put in just the right place. Tell Archie, "Spiders are one of God's most orderly creatures."

    b.   Remind Archie that God requires him be orderly too. Spiders have orderly webs. Children must have orderly bedrooms and school desks.

    c.   The best way to help Archie practice cleaning his room is to write down specifically what constitutes cleaning his room. For example, make the bed, put dirty laundry in the hamper, put shoes on shoe rack, clean clothes must be put in the proper drawer, video games and DVDs are to be kept in the compartment under the television. Post the instructions in his bedroom in a conspicuous place.

2) School: Archie has a messy desk.

    a.   Archie's parents should purchase a binder for him. It should be divided into sections for each subject. Put a label on each section that corresponds with the subject. For example, reading, math or English. When Archie gets homework assignments for a particular subject he immediately puts them in the proper section of the binder. He would also put returned assignments, tests that need to be signed, study guides or flash cards in the appropriate section of the binder.

    b.   Parents should buy a pencil pouch that fits in the binder.

    c.   The parents should check the binder and pencil pouch on a daily basis. This is not the obligation of Archie's school teacher. This is what godly parenting is all about (Deuteronomy 6:5-9, Ephesians 6:1-4, Proverbs 22:6). This is part of teaching Archie wisdom as it pertains to organization (Proverbs 1:2-5). Bringing his binder home every afternoon must be a rule that when violated has disciplinary consequences.

3) Personal appearance: Archie needs get in the habit of bathing every night or in the morning. He needs to brush his teeth at least once a day and he must comb his hair. When he is old enough, he will need to use deodorant everyday. All the buttons on his shirt must be buttoned and his clothes should be clean and neat.

The DSM says "often does not follow through on instructions and fails to finish school work, chores, or duties in the workplace."

Archie tends to be a quitter. He does not finish tasks except for those he is interested in and enjoys. Archie has two sinful habits or attitudes of thinking. First, he doesn't obey his parents or teachers. Second, he does not finish projects or assignments. Archie is being selfish and irresponsible. He must repent and seek forgiveness from God and neighbor (parents and teacher).

Archie must be taught he cannot "despise wisdom and instruction" (Proverbs 1:7) if he is going to please God. He needs to learn that behaving responsibly and completing a task is important to God. Jesus said, "I glorified you on the earth, having accomplished the work which you have given Me to do" (John 17:4). The apostle Paul said, "I have fought the good fight, I have finished the course, I have kept the faith" (2 Timothy 4:7). Jesus said to his disciples, "My food is to do the will of Him who sent Me and to accomplish His work" John 4:34).

Questions to Ask:

"What is Archie's goal? "

1) Does Archie not complete a task because he doesn't *feel* like it and he wants to do something else?

2) Does Archie quit in the middle of an assignment because of *laziness*?

Archie needs to learn to discipline himself. He needs to understand God doesn't want him to live by his feelings. He should live by "every word that proceeds out of the mouth of God" (Matthew 4:4). Archie does many things he doesn't feel like doing. For example, he goes to school, brushes his teeth, cleans his room, etc. However, he only wants to obey God when he feels like obeying God.

Putting-Off and Putting-On

"For consider Him who has endured such hostility by sinners against Himself, so that you will not grow weary and lose heart" (Hebrews 12:3). The put-off is "growing weary and losing heart." The put-on is "endurance." Make seven or eight copies of the put-off and put-on verse. Make the font large enough so it can be read from a distance. Post the put-off and put-on verse in various places around the house. Quiz Archie in the morning and evening on his put-off and put-on verse.

Practicing the Put-On (Righteousness)

Archie's sin is certainly not unique. Temptations such as this are "common to man" (1 Corinthians 10:13). All Christians must guard against giving up when things are difficult. The path of a Christian does not always lead him through green pastures and beside still waters. These exercises will help Archie practice perseverance (endurance).

Homework – A

1) Refer to Prayer and Repentance above / Homework A

Homework – B

2) Be an example for Archie. Have you promised Archie you would do something and did not follow through and do it? Do you have unfinished projects around the house?

Homework – C

1) The parents must teach Archie to "consider" Jesus when discussing perseverance.

2) Ask Archie, "Was Jesus ever tempted to give up and not complete his work?" Tell Archie how Jesus became "very distressed and troubled" (Mark 14:33) and "deeply grieved" (verse 34) as his suffering for all our sins loomed nearer. Jesus asked His Father to remove this cup of suffering from Him. Jesus was tempted to give up and not finish His work.

3) Ask Archie, "What if Jesus had given up?" If Jesus had given up then Archie's sins could not be forgiven. He would have no Savior (1 Corinthians 15:14). Show Archie in the Bible how others were tempted to give up, but persevered. For example, Paul was shipwrecked, imprisoned and abandoned by all his friends. Joseph, as a teenager, was sold into slavery by his brothers. People laughed at Noah who was building a boat on dry land.

4) Ask Archie, "What did Jesus do when he was tempted to give up?" Even though He was tempted to quit, Jesus finished His work. He continued to think of what God wanted Him to do and not what He wanted to do. He remained focused on the task at hand. Jesus did not give up (John 17:4).

5) Give Archie a book that he would be able to read in about 30 minutes. Tell him to practice his put-on (being like Jesus) by reading the whole book from the beginning to the end without stopping. If his attention drifts and he is tempted to give up remind him to think of his put-off and put-on verse. When he is finished, ask him to tell you about the book.

6) You may give him some math problems, or other assignments to practice his put-off and put-on.

Hyperactivity Category

The DSM says "Often fidgets with hands or feet or squirms in seat. Often leaves seat in classroom or in other situations in which remaining seated are expected. Often runs about or climbs excessively in situations in which it is inappropriate. Often has difficulty playing or engaging in leisure activities quietly. Is often "on the go" or often acts as if "driven by a motor." Often talks excessively.

The problem in all of the issues above is self-control. The Bible clearly teaches that Christ's disciples are to be people who exercise restraint over their impulses and desires. Unfortunately, in a culture immersed in psychology, people are told and believe they cannot control themselves. Someone has said, "Teenagers are going to have sex. You cannot stop them." Teenagers are viewed as not being able to master their desires. However, Joseph, a teenager living far from home refused to sin against God, Potifar, Potifar's wife, and his own body (Genesis 39:12, 1 Corinthians 6:18). Daniel, a teenager, rejected the delicious food from the king's table because it had been offered to idols (Daniel 1:8). They exercised self-control because not to do so was sinful.

Solomon says a man who has no self-control is like a city whose walls have fallen down (Proverbs 25:28). If the walls are destroyed the city is defenseless. When the walls of Jericho fell the army of Israel easily invaded and conquered the city. Just as a city without walls is vulnerable to its enemies, a person without self-control is vulnerable to all kinds of temptations and sins. People of all ages pay a heavy price when they fail to exercise self-control over their desires, impulses, and emotions.

James says of all the parts of the human body the tongue is the most difficult to control. It is impossible for a horseman to control his steed without a bit in its mouth. In like manner without a bridle on the tongue no man can control himself aright. The tongue can defile the entire body (James 3:6). It breeds and gives vent to every sort of sinful craving and appetite. A Christian who can learn to keep his tongue under control is able to curb the passions and desires of his whole body as well (James 3:2). Although the tongue is reckless and full of deadly poison, it can be tamed with God's help. Archie's parents must prayerfully lead Archie in practicing the control of his tongue. Archie needs to learn there is a "time to be silent and a time to speak" (Ecclesiastes 3:7). Solomon warns, "When there are many words, transgression is unavoidable, but he who restrains his lips is wise" (Proverbs 10:19). The person who fails to control his tongue is always getting into trouble.

Question to Ask

1) "Is Archie's goal to please God or self?"

Archie must be taught that pleasing God includes exercising self-control over the parts of his body (hands, arms, legs, mouth, etc.). His parents must help him to learn self-control. Again, this is part of godly parenting. This is not the responsibility of Archie's school teacher.

Putting-Off and Putting-On

Paul said, "I discipline my body and make it my slave" (1 Corinthians 9:27). The put-off that is implied is "not to discipline my body." The put-on is "I discipline my body and make it a slave." Another put-off and put-on is in Galatians 5. Verses 19-21 include a list of desires that are called "deeds of the flesh." The words at the end of verse 21 "and things like these" imply the list is not exhaustive, but only examples. All behaviors that are unruly, uncooperative, disruptive, etc. would be considered "deeds of the flesh." The put-off would be "deeds of the flesh." The put-on is "the fruit of the

Spirit...self-control" (verse 22-23). The put-off and put-on for the tongue is Proverbs 10:19, "When there are many words, transgression is unavoidable, but he who restrains his lips is wise." The put-off is "many words." The put-on "restrains his lips." Make seven or eight copies of the put-off and put-on verse. Make the font large enough so it can be read from a distance. Post the put-off and put-on verse in various places around the house. Quiz Archie in the morning and evening on his put-off and put-on verse.

Practicing the Put-On (Righteousness)

Self-control is a spiritual discipline. Like every discipline, self-control must be practiced if it is to become a habit.

Homework – A

1) Refer to Prayer and Repentance above / Homework A

Homework – B

2) Teach Archie by example. Do you model self-control or do you have "outburst of anger?" (Galatians 5:20). Are you "impatient?" (Galatians 5:22). Does Archie witness you and your spouse arguing and "losing your cool?"

Homework – C

1) Explain to Archie a slave is a person who is owned by another person (the master or boss). He is not free to come and go when he wants. A slave cannot own his own house. He lives in a slave's house behind his master's house. A slave works long and hard for his master. He does whatever the master commands. He does not get paid. He can never leave the master unless he is sold to another master.

2) Ask Archie if he would like to be someone's slave? Why wouldn't he want to be a slave?

3) The apostle Paul says you can be a slave to the desires of your own body. Read 1 Corinthians 9:27. Ask Archie if he is a slave to certain feelings and desires of his body? Does his body control him? It should be the other way around. His body should be his slave. He needs to be the master of his body and not allow his body be the master of him.

4) Paul wrote, "Each one looking to yourself, so that you too will not be tempted" (Galatians 6:1). Ask Archie, "Where are you most

tempted to lose self-control?" Help Archie identify the situations where he is tempted to allow his body to be the master and he is the slave. For example, there are certain subjects Archie may not like and is more prone to fidget and be disruptive. At home around the dinner table may also be a temptation for Archie. Teach Archie to stay alert, be on his guard and pray. Jesus told the disciples in their time of temptation "Keep watching and praying that you may not enter into temptation; the spirit (Archie's inner man that wants to obey God) is willing, but the flesh (the outer man habituated to lack of self-control or sin) is weak" (Matthew 26:41).

Homework – D

1) Read 1 Corinthians 9:24. "Do you not know that those who run in a race all run, but only one receives the prize? Run in such a way that you may win." Just as it takes practice to be a good athlete and win a race or a game it takes practice to discipline one's body. It even takes practice to be good at a video game.

2) Remind Archie of the hot days and effort he put forth playing on the little league baseball team. He practiced batting, fielding, and running the bases. Learning to master a video game takes intense concentration and focus too. Remind him how he failed to beat the game, but kept on putting forth an effort until he mastered it.

3) Ask Archie "What do these verses say about self-control?" Galatians 5:22-23; 2 Timothy 3:1-6

Homework – F

1) Read Proverbs 21:23. Ask Archie what kind of trouble he has gotten into because he has failed to guard his mouth? Ask him "Were you showing honor to the person speaking? Did your behavior please God?" Explain to him the sowing and reaping principle of cause and effect (Galatians 6:7-9).

Homework – G

1) Tell Archie he can learn self control if he puts forth the effort and prays for God's help. Others have put-on the righteous habit of self-control. Noah did not become angry when people made fun of him when he was building the ark. Joseph was not vengeful toward his brothers who had been mean to him and sold him into slavery. Daniel would not eat the delicious food offered to idols.

2) Read 2 Peter 1:6. Ask Archie what the eight qualities are that he should be increasing in as a believer?

3) Remind Archie of God's promises. Read together the following verses: Philippians 4:13; 1 Corinthians 10:13; John 14:14.

Impulsivity Category

Often blurts out answers before questions have been completed. Often has difficulty waiting turn. Often interrupts or intrudes on others (e.g., butts into conversations or games).

People are selfish. For that reason Jesus carefully warned His followers of the dangers of pride and selfishness. Jesus repeatedly emphasized the fact that self is the problem and self-denial is the pathway to true godliness. In coming into the world to do the Father's will, Jesus' concern for others was so intense that He "forgot Himself." The Lord did His work so wholeheartedly that He was not even aware of Himself. Even when His work for the day was done, Jesus retreated into solitude where He became "lost" in communion with God the Father.

Before the Fall, Adam and Eve were other-oriented; their focus was on God and each other; self was never an issue. All of the evil, wickedness, and ruin that came from sin resulted in man's turning from doing God's will to doing his own will. As Isaiah 53:6 says, "We all, like sheep, have gone astray, each of us has turned to his own *way*" (italics ours). Ever since the intrusion of sin into the world, man has been self-oriented. Selfishness became the natural disposition of man's sinful heart.[19]

Selfishness or self-centeredness is a major issue in people who have been labeled Attention Deficit Hyperactive Disorder, Oppositional Defiant Disorder and other so called behavioral disorders. Archie does not pay attention to the responsibilities and obligations God required of him. His focus is on doodling in his notebook, whispering to the person in the seat across from him, playing with his pencils, staring out the window, etc., instead of listening to his teacher. He loses his pencil and eraser because he is careless and thoughtless. He is inconsiderate of his parents who take great pains to buy him the necessary things he needed for school. He either does not do his homework or he fails to finish it. He would rather do things that interest him like watching

---

[19] For further study in the self-oriented lifestyle verses the other-oriented lifestyle (focus on God and neighbor) see David Tyler's book *Jesus Christ: Self-Denial or Self-Esteem* published by Timeless Texts. (IBSN 1-889032-36-0).

television or playing video games. He fidgets in his seat, interrupts others and will not wait his turn. Archie is selfish. Selfishness is not a disease.

Questions to Ask

"What is Archie's goal and purpose?" Archie's goal may be...

1) To say or do what he wants because he has other things to do?

2) To say or do what he wants because he wants to be first?

3) To say or do what he wants because he wants gratification now?

Putting-Off and Putting-On

Archie would let his personal interests govern his behavior. His "me first" attitude coupled with impatience lead to rude and selfish behavior. Paul wrote, "Do nothing from selfishness or empty conceit, but with humility of mind regard one another as more important than yourselves" (Philippians 2:3). The put-off is selfishness and the put-on is humility. Make seven or eight copies of the put-off and put-on verse. Make the font large enough so it can be read from a distance. Post the put-off and put-on verse in various places around the house. Quiz Archie in the morning and evening on his put-off and put-on verse.

Practicing the Put-On (Righteousness)

Homework – A

1) Refer to Prayer and Repentance above / Homework A

Homework – B

2) Teach Archie by example. Do you interrupt Archie when he is speaking? Does Archie witness you interrupting or behaving in a selfish way toward your spouse or others?

3) Ask Archie, "What is humility?" Paul says humility is to, "regard one another as more important than yourselves," (Philippians 2:3) Regarding another person as more important than yourself identifies the method or strategy by which Archie would practice humility. It is the parent's task to help Archie focus upon God and neighbor, rather than self. The assignment of performing three

acts of kindness every day is how he can practice humility.

4) Record acts of kindness in a journal every day. For example, Tuesday, January 15 1) At home. "I waited patiently until mother got off the phone to ask for a cookie." 2) At school. "I waited patiently in the cafeteria line at school." 3) At school. "I allowed another boy to get ahead of me in line."

Homework – C

1) "Each one looking to yourself, so that you too will not be tempted" (Galatians 6:1). Ask Archie when and where he is most tempted to be impatient or selfish. For example, during the lunch period, the teacher has reported that Archie does not walk to the cafeteria in an orderly fashion. He gets out of line and is disruptive. Also he interrupts when his mother is talking with someone on the phone.

2) Explain to Archie how he does not want to become a slave to selfishness (Romans 6:16). God wants Archie to focus on self-denial in order to please God and be a blessing to others. Jesus said, "Whoever wishes to become great among you shall be your servant, and whoever wishes to be first among you shall be your slave" Matthew 20:26-27).

5) Archie is to have the same attitude as Jesus. Explain to him how Jesus' attitude blessed him by providing salvation. Read Philippians 2:3-9. Just like Jesus, Archie is not merely to look out for his own personal interests (as he was in the habit of doing), but for the interests of others. Archie's goal is to have the mind and attitude of Christ.

Homework – D

1) God holds Archie responsible for his sinful behavior. Warn Archie that he needs to be watchful, alert and prayerful so he doesn't fall into temptation.

2) Remind Archie that godliness takes great effort on his part. He must also be prayerfully asking God for strength in times of temptation.

It is important for parents and counselors to realize that the assignments and suggestions above are not simply yet another shallow strategy intended to change behavior in the short term. To be sincere in what we are attempting to do we must acknowledge that this change is far deeper than having Archie bathe daily, pay attention in class, stop fidgeting and interrupting, and start finishing his homework. Archie has a lifetime ahead of him whose foundation is being laid day by precious day. Parents often get nostalgic over how fast their children grew up and were gone. The time for action is now! It is not the exclusive responsibility of the school system, the physician, the Pastor or the Sunday school teacher.   No, it is the responsibility of parents to parent and do it biblically.

The biblical change discussed above involves putting off unrighteousness and putting on righteousness. Children do not possess the discipline to take on such a monumental task alone. However, they are incredibly pliable according to what they observe and what they are taught. They are in a prime time in their lives to develop who they will become. Regular, consistent, loving, Scriptural guidance from parents is essential. Occasionally, the potter will use a simple tool to shape a lump of clay into the vessel he desires it to be. Parents have an opportunity to be that tool as the Potter molds the clay into His very special image. While God can work miracles in any life at any time, affording children the best possible foundation, built on the Solid Rock of Scripture, gives them the best opportunity to live a productive, fruit-bearing, kingdom-oriented life that is honoring to their parents, and more importantly, honoring to Almighty God.

Chapter 4
The Heart of the Matter

Watch over your heart with all diligence, for from it
flow the springs of life.
Solomon, *Proverbs 4:23*

Foolishness is bound up in the heart of a child...
Solomon, *Proverbs 22:15*

This people honors Me with their lips, but their
heart is far away from Me.
Jesus Christ, *Matthew 15:8*

When looking at the core behaviors associated with ADHD
(hyperactivity, impulsiveness, inattention) and all the associated
behaviors stemming from these (talking out of turn, wandering around
the classroom, forgetfulness, etc.), parents often wonder, "what can I
do?" While the answer to that question is not simple, per se, it is
not outside of the normal scope of good, biblical parenting. In other
words, the answer is easy, but the application of the answer is where
things get a bit more challenging.

In chapter 8, *The Human Mind,* we will show that all of our
behaviors flow from the heart. The heart is the inner person, only
seen by the person himself and God. In the unregenerate man, it is
evil, through and through. In the regenerated man, it is gloriously
renewed by the power of the Holy Spirit to reclaim its original form
fully in the image and likeness of God. As a parent, the keys to
unlocking the heart of the matter in ADHD are data gathering and
discernment. It is talking WITH Archie as opposed to talking TO him.
Ultimately, as a parent, what you are attempting to determine (data
gathering) through talking with Archie are the motives (discernment)
flowing from Archie's heart. You are gathering data about what he is
thinking and feeling while observing his behavior. Are his motives
(thinking and feeling) sinful thus leading to sinful behavior? Are

they selfish, jealous, idolatrous, angry, rebellious, envious, etc.? What are those motives doing (behavior)? By observing Archie's behavior and gathering data about his thinking and feeling, you can discern the motives of his heart. To know Archie's heart is to understand his thinking, his feelings, and his behavior because each one of these flows from that very same heart.

One note of caution: to avoid being selfish as a parent, you must realize this is not about you. How *YOU* feel about Archie's behavior is not the issue. How *YOU* are viewed by others is not the issue. "Where have *I* gone wrong?" is the wrong question to be asking. *YOU* are not what is playing on the main screen in the theatre of the Universe. This is about Archie and his relationship with Jesus Christ. Archie's heart and what is flowing from it is the issue.

After practicing data gathering and determining the disposition of Archie's heart through biblical discernment, you have, in effect, arrived at an accurate, biblical diagnosis of Archie's behavior. Now, you can go about a treatment plan designed not only to affect Archie's behavior, but also to teach him lifelong lessons based on Scripture (discipleship). Simply changing Archie's behavior through positive and negative reinforcement techniques is not enough. You are after something deeper. You (and God!) are after a changed heart.

First and foremost, the gospel must be applied liberally and often. Archie is naïve and immature, but he is still a sinner. He was born into the fallen line of Adam and is made in Adam's likeness and according to his image (Genesis 5:3). Remember that no matter what you as a parent do; Archie was "bad" or fallen from his birth. Archie is not bad because of what you have or have not done; rather he is bad because of his "lostness." Biblical parenting can mitigate some of that "badness" through changing his behavior externally but it will never substitute for salvation! Your effort is much more profound than just changing Archie's behavior. In fact, changing behavior without a changed heart is the pinnacle of hypocrisy. Jesus spoke to this very issue in Matthew 15:1-20.

Based on your data gathering, you will next *apply* biblical discernment. Your primary goal in dealing with the behaviors labeled as ADHD is to bring Archie's sin to light. Explain his sin in terms he can understand. Tell him he is wrong not just in the eyes of Mom or Dad, but also, and more importantly, in the eyes of Almighty God.

46

Explain the difference between his behavior which is unrighteous and the biblical alternative which is righteous. If his behavior is habitual, introduce him to the put-off/put-on teaching covered in chapters 3 and 11. In essence, you are teaching Archie to draw out the motivation for his behavior (Proverbs 20:5), discern whether or not it is sinful or righteous and act upon it accordingly.

If Archie is saved, by the power of the indwelling Holy Spirit, applying Scripture to Archie's heart will allow him to begin to change. His heart will shift from unrighteous to righteous in that particular area. When his heart changes, it will lead to changed thinking, feelings and behavior. It is through this sanctification process that God slowly and progressively makes believers more and more into the likeness of Christ.[20] [21] [22] [23] Table 1 on the following page should be helpful in data gathering and discernment.

---

[20] Lou Priolo, *Teach Them Diligently: How to Use the Scriptures in Child Training* (Woodruff, S.C.: Timeless Texts, 2000).

[21] John MacArthur, *What the Bible Says About Parenting: God's Plan for Rearing Your Child* (Nashville, TN.: Word Publishing, 2000).

[22] Tedd Tripp, *Shepherding a Child's Heart* (Wapwallopen, PA.: Shepherd Press, 1995).

[23] Ginger Plowman, *Don't Make Me Count to Three* (Wapwallopen, PA.: Shepherd Press, 2003)

Table 1

ADHD Behavior	Example	Possible Heart Issues	Related Scripture References [24]
	Blurts out answers; has difficulty waiting; interrupts or intrudes	Foolishness and folly, self-control, rebellion; careless talk	Psalm 19:14 Proverbs 1:7; 3:35; 10:1; 12:15,18; 14:3; 15:5,28,32; 16:20; 17:11; 18:13,15; 19:26; 21:23; 25:28; 26:11-12; 29:1,11,20; 30:17 Ephesians 4:29; 5:4 Colossians 4:6 James 1:2-5, 26 Galatians 5:7-11,22-23 I Peter 1:13-15; 2:19-23 2 Peter 1:5-6 Genesis 3:6-7 Hebrews 3:7-19 1 Samuel 15:22-25 Daniel 9:5-19 Joshua 24:14-15 Titus 2:11-12 Deuteronomy 21:18-21
	Fidgets or squirms; leaves seat at inappropriate times; runs or climbs excessively; always "on-the-go"; talks excessively	Impatience, disobedience, self-control	Galatians 5:22-23 James 1:2-5; 5:7-11 I Peter 1:13-15; 2:19-23 Titus 2:11-12 2 Peter 1:5-6 Proverbs 1:8-9,18:13,15; 25:28; 29:11,20 Genesis 3:6-7 Exodus 20:12 Ephesians 6:1-3 Colossians 3:20
Inattention	Makes careless mistakes in school-work; fails to finish work or chores; does not listen; often loses things; is forgetful	Uncontrolled thoughts, easily influenced to sin; foolishness and folly; laziness and slothfulness	Proverbs 1:7,10; 3:35; 6:6-11; 10:1,4-5; 12:15; 13:4; 14:3,23; 15:5; 16:20; 18:9; 24:30-34; 26:11-12; 31:10-31 2 Thessalonians 4:3-5 2 Timothy 2:22 Mark 7:21-13 Romans 12:2 2 Corinthians 10:4-5 Philippians 4:8 Daniel 1:8 Galatians 5:1 Ephesians 4:14; 6:10-18 Hebrews 4:14-16; 10:23 James 1:8; 4:17 1 Corinthians 10:13; 15:58

---

[24] Armand P. Tiffe, *Transformed Into His Likeness: A Handbook for Putting off Sin and Putting on Righteousness* (Bemidji, MN.: Focusing Publishing, 2005).

A Mini-Case Illustration

On a nice April afternoon, Archie quickly makes his way home from school. Upon arriving, he finds his mom in the kitchen talking on the telephone. Archie approaches her and, in a normal voice asks if he can have a snack. His mom is sitting at the table with a pencil and paper. Still on the phone, she looks at him sternly and does not respond. In a louder voice, Archie again asks if he can have a snack. His mom puts her hand over the telephone mouthpiece and tells him to wait until she is off the telephone. Unsatisfied with her answer, Archie trumpets in a loud voice, "I want cookies, I want cookies, I want cookies!" What is a parent to do?

Option 1

Archie's mom again puts her hand over the phone and tells him he is going to have to wait and if he screams again, he will go to his room with no snack and will not be allowed to come out until dinner time. She is on a very important call and does not want the person on the other end to hear him yelling!

Option 2

Archie's mom concludes her call and has Archie sit down at the kitchen table. She reminds herself of Psalm 127:3 and quietly asks Archie what he wants. He says he wants cookies. She asks Archie if he noticed she was involved in an important telephone call. He says yes, but he was really hungry because he did not like the school lunch today. He did not eat much and has been hungry all afternoon. He says he was really, really hungry and that he ran all the way home from school thinking about something to eat.

From this short conversation (data gathering) and from observing Archie's behavior, Archie's Mom has determined (discerned) his behaviors were:

- <u>Disobedient</u>: interrupting, persisting in asking after "the look" and after being told to wait until she was off the telephone
- <u>Rebellious</u>: repeatedly screaming, "I want cookies" when he did not get his way immediately
- <u>Lacking self-control</u>: He saw her on the phone and would not wait until she was finished to make his request

She shares this with Archie telling him that not only was his behavior wrong and unacceptable in her eyes, but they were also wrong and unacceptable in the sight of God. Archie sinned against her and he has sinned against God. He needs to seek her forgiveness and that of God as well.

Archie, looking at the floor, tells her he is sorry. She again corrects him and tells him being sorry is not enough. He needs to ask for forgiveness because being sorry is all about Archie while asking for forgiveness is about the person who was offended. Archie, still looking at the floor, asks her to forgive him. She grants forgiveness and encourages Archie to pray, asking for God's forgiveness as well, which he does.

While Archie is still sitting, teary-eyed, at the table, she goes to the refrigerator and takes out a tub of yogurt and gets a small bowl of granola, giving it to Archie as his snack. She also opens her Bible and shares James 5:7-11 and talks with Archie about patience and self-control. She explains that she has prepared his snack in advance because she knew the lunch being served today was not one of his favorites. The telephone call she received was important, but unexpected. She then turns to Colossians 3:20, reads the verse to Archie:

> **"Children, be obedient to your parents in all things,
> for this is well-pleasing to the Lord."**

She asks Archie if his behavior while she was on the telephone represented the obedience spoken of in the verse. Was his behavior pleasing in the sight of God? He says no, still intent on finishing his snack. She asks him to explain what, specifically, about his behavior was disobedient. He responds that he should not have yelled, "I want cookies!" and that he probably should not have even interrupted her call in the first place. He should have been more patient. She tells him that his interrupting after being told not to do so was indeed disobedient, it was wrong, and it was a sin. She then explains that his yelling was not necessarily disobedience, as much as it was rebellion.

Turning to the warning given in Proverbs 29:1 she explains that Archie's rebellion will have severe consequences not just now, but also in the future:

> **"A man who hardens his neck after much reproof
> will suddenly be broken beyond remedy."**

50

Lastly, she moves over to sit by Archie and turns to Philippians 2:3-4 and asks him to read it:

"Do nothing from selfishness or empty conceit, but with humility of mind let each of you regard one another as more important than himself; do not merely look out for your own personal interests, but also for the interests of others."

They discuss selfishness and how God directs us to put others before ourselves. Yes, Archie was hungry when he got home, but if he were putting his Mom before himself and his wants, he would have had a much easier time waiting a few brief moments for her to finish her call before asking for a snack.

Chapter 5
What Else Could It Be?

"Distracted? Disorganized? Frustrated? Modern
Life or Adult ADD? Many adults have been living
with Adult attention deficit disorder (Adult ADD)
and don't recognize it. Why? Because its symptoms
are often mistaken for stressful life."
> Eli Lilly & Company advertisement
> for Strattera,
> *U.S. News and World Report,*
> April 26, 2004, p.65

"Do not love the world nor the things in the world.
If anyone loves the world, the love of the Father is
not in him. For all that is in the world, the lust of the
flesh and the lust of the eyes and the boastful pride
of life, is not from the Father, but is from the world."
> Apostle John
> 1 John 2:15-16 NASU

Part of the job of a physician is to correctly diagnose the problem
a patient has presented. It is often like detective work. The physician
uses all of the tools at his or her disposal to arrive at the correct answer.
Preliminarily, these tools include what the patient tells the physician
about what they are feeling and what the physician observes using
sight, touch, hearing, and even smell. Further tools may include
laboratory tests, x-rays or other scans, and biopsies or tissue samples.
Sometimes, the physician can administer written tests to evaluate a
patient's thinking ability or other mental functions. Of course, the
physician also possesses experience and a knowledge of his or her
patients which in and of itself is invaluable.

The patient usually has a primary problem, a sore throat or a
fever, for example, and this is known as the chief complaint. It is
the launching point from which the physician begins the task of
diagnosing. Taking that chief complaint, the patient's medical history

and other observations the physician has made in the first few moments of the examination, the physician begins to formulate the full realm of possible diagnoses. This is known as the differential diagnosis and involves systematically comparing the patient's signs and symptoms to known diseases or problems, and confirming or eliminating certain diseases or problems based on the patients signs and symptoms and the subsequent examination.

For example, there are literally hundreds of problems that could result in a fever so when a patient has a fever, more information is needed for a proper diagnosis. How high is the fever? Is it constant or does it come and go? What other medical problems does the patient have? What other symptoms does the patient have? All these, and many other questions must be answered in order to arrive at a correct diagnosis. In short, the differential diagnosis is the process of comparing the signs, symptoms, objective observations, blood tests, x-rays or other types of scans, patient social and medical history, physical examination, and a host of other variables in order to narrow the diagnosis. All this is coupled with the physician's experience, knowledge of the patient and professional judgment in order to arrive at the final diagnosis.

Why is the diagnosis so important? It almost sounds silly to ask such a question. However, a correct diagnosis is absolutely critical to assuring the proper treatment is given. Is the fever from bacterial meningitis which requires immediate high-dose antibiotics to save the patient's life or is it a common viral infection that will resolve in a few days with rest and fluids? That is an extreme example, but it highlights the importance of the correct diagnosis. It causes one to pause and ponder the power of a diagnosis.

The diagnosis is a very powerful instrument in medicine; perhaps the most powerful. A correct diagnosis may save your life while an incorrect diagnosis could cost you dearly. An incorrect diagnosis could lead to unnecessary expensive or painful procedures or drug treatment. It could delay the correct treatment as well. Beyond that, a misdiagnosis could have health or life insurance implications for years to come. Much is at stake in the business of diagnosis.

Differential Diagnosis: ADHD

On the surface, it would seem that the diagnosis of ADHD would be straightforward. Oftentimes, it is treated as such. The school demands the parents take the child to the school's approved physician; the child is seen once and a prescription for a stimulant drug follows. The prescription is filled and little Archie joins the ranks of his medicated peers. His behavior improves and everyone at school is satisfied. What is the problem? There was no effort to make a differential diagnosis. The diagnosis was made in a cursory fashion based on the "close working relationship" between school officials and the referral physician. The physician relied on the subjective assessment of school personnel and a single appointment to diagnose Archie with ADHD. He made assumptions that may or may not be rooted in sound medical science. Is it even remotely possible a misdiagnosis has occurred?

What else could it be? Table 1 contains a brief description related to the ADHD core symptoms.

Table 1

ADHD Core Symptom	What Else Could It Be?
Impulsivity	Thyroid disorders, hearing problems, anxiety, high intelligence, substance abuse
Inattention	Seizures, diabetes, sleep disorders, vision problems, alternative learning style, depression
Hyperactivity	Asthma or other medications, lead poisoning, diet, caffeine intake, mild mental retardation

If we consider the differential diagnosis of suspected ADHD, we see there are many alternatives to be considered prior to confirming the diagnosis. In addition to meeting the criteria outlined in the DSM-IV-TR, the physician must also consider the possibility of any number of the disorders and problems listed below in Table 2. The alternative diagnoses in this table reflect input from a wide number of sources and while the authors do not consider all of the "conditions" listed to be diseases in the classic sense, the objective is to show how many other possibilities exist for behavior that is labeled ADHD. A hasty diagnosis leads to hasty and perhaps unneeded or even dangerous treatments. Most of the other disorders and problems listed would not respond well to amphetamine treatment. For example, if Archie needed glasses, powerful stimulant drugs would not help him see any better. However, he will no longer be a disruption in the classroom, even though he still cannot see the board. The school system is satisfied because his behavior has improved, but his ability to learn has not been impacted. In fact, it may have been stifled even further.

Everyone involved has failed Archie starting with his parents, his teachers, his school system, and his physician. This has all occurred because of tunnel vision. Assumptions are made and treated as absolute truth. A diagnosis is made, treatment follows and everyone is happy…except Archie.

Table 2

Medical Disorders	Medical Disorders
Asthma	Substance abuse
Infection	Rare disorders
Seizures	• Aarskog syndrome
Diabetes	• Chromosome 17,
Thyroid disease	trisomy p11.2
Vision problems	• Fragile X syndrome
Hearing problems	• Soto's syndrome
Environmental allergies	• Williams syndrome
Anemia (iron deficiency)	Sleep disorders
Head injury or brain trauma	• Restless leg syndrome
Vitamin or mineral deficiencies	• Sleep apnea
Lead or other heavy metal poisoning	Medication side effects

Behavioral Disorders	Disorders of Development
Chronic fear Schizophrenia Mood disorders Bipolar disorder Adjustment disorder Post-traumatic stress disorder Depression (20% of ADHD patients) Anxiety disorders (25% of ADHD patients) Conduct disorder (25-50% of ADHD patients) Tourette's syndrome (70% with tics have ADHD) Oppositional defiant disorder (33% of ADHD patients)	Dysgraphia Learning style Mild mental retardation Fetal alcohol syndrome Exposure to drugs in utero Autism/Asperger's syndrome Reactive attachment disorder Pervasive developmental disorder Perceptual or processing disorders Speech and language disorders (10-15% have ADHD)
Social Problems	**Other**
Poor social skills Child abuse or neglect Stressful home environment Inadequate or poor parenting English as a second language Inappropriate educational setting or level Classroom dynamics – unsafe or disruptive	Dietary considerations • Caffeine • Food allergies • Raw or refined sugar High intelligence/gifted Normal childhood behavior

The proper work-up for a physician considering an ADHD diagnosis includes substantial effort at ruling out any number of other disorders or problems before arriving at the ADHD diagnosis. A complete medical history, including that of the mother's pregnancy, is the starting point followed by a complete and thorough physical examination, including an assessment of coordination and motor skills. A thorough family history should be obtained as well for background information. The child's current home and school environment should be assessed in *great* detail as should any previous educational, achievement, speech, and language testing results. A mental status evaluation should be completed to test cognition and memory.

If warranted based on the history and physical findings, blood tests for heavy metals, thyroid function, HIV and Lyme diseases, and genetic screening should be performed. An electroencephalogram (EEG) to rule out seizures, a sleep study, and brain scans may also be considered, again based on the history and physical findings. In addition, there are several behaviorally based rating scales that can be administered to children, parents and teachers to predict or disprove a diagnosis of ADHD. These can be complementary in arriving at the diagnosis, though they should not be used as the exclusive tool.

The bottom line is that a diagnosis of ADHD should not be an in-and-out process. A ten minute appointment followed by a prescription for a stimulant drug should be looked upon with great suspicion. While most parents are not physicians or even medical professionals, common sense dictates that before you consent to placing your child on any medication, you expect the physician to be very thorough and comprehensive in arriving at the diagnosis and in choosing a treatment. A diagnosis of ADHD is significant and has far reaching consequences. It should *not* be arrived upon based on the subjective assessment of teachers, social workers or school psychologists. The responsibility for ruling out ADHD lies squarely on the shoulders of a patient's parents and a thorough physician who assure that all other possibilities are eliminated. In addition, the physician should also be quick to discuss the various treatment options with the patient and the parents, rather than immediately reaching for the prescription pad. A Christian physician should also have a different perspective based on the addition of Scriptural principles to his practice.

If Archie does not have any of the host of other possible "legitimate" disorders and everything else is deemed to be "normal," Scripture would have a completely different diagnosis of Archie's behavior, thinking and feelings than a label of ADHD. Scripture's diagnosis would include sins like selfishness, impatience, lack of self-control, rebellion and the like. Amphetamine drugs are not the answer for treating these spiritual conditions and may even make some of the behaviors worse. Confession, repentance, restitution and putting off old behaviors are the treatment of choice along with putting on selflessness, humility, submission, self-control and a host of others. Archie does not need drugs to treat his sinfulness, he needs a Savior.

Adult ADHD: The Disease of the Distracted Procrastinator

He who gathers in summer is a son who acts wisely, but he who sleeps in harvest is a son who acts shamefully (Proverbs 10:5 NASU).

Adult ADHD is a fairly new diagnosis, rising in prominence and public awareness coincidentally just before Eli Lilly and Company received marketing approval for Strattera[R] to "treat" adult ADHD. In their book entitled, *Selling Sickness*, Moynihan and Cassels say,

> "Vince Parry's insights into how pharmaceutical companies help to shape public perceptions about [medical] conditions are invaluable, because the strategies are often hidden from public view. Men and women like him with expertise in advertising, marketing, and public relations working from chic offices in Manhattan, London, Toronto, and Sydney are being paid to fundamentally change the way we think about our bodies, our health, and the conditions we supposedly suffer. The pro-drug messages hammered out in these marketing offices are camouflaged as 'awareness-raising' exercises and then transmitted far and wide, through massive advertising campaigns, sponsored medical education, and PR [public relations] campaigns that generate much media reporting,"[25]

According to several literature sources, adult ADHD affects 30-70% of those who had ADHD as a child, meaning up to 5% of the adult population of the United States is allegedly affected. As expected, diagnosing adult ADHD is difficult because the hallmark symptoms (inattention, irritability, distractibility, impulsivity) are also found in a number of other conditions such as depression and substance abuse[26]. These habits of behavior are also discussed throughout Scripture as sins and not medical conditions or diseases.

Medically speaking, the chief complaint is often either poor concentration or inattention and, thanks to the massive advertising

---

[25] R. Moynihan, & A, Cassels, *Selling Sickness: How the World's Biggest Pharmaceutical Companies Are Turning Us All Into Patients* (New York, NY.: Nation Books, 2005), p. 71

[26] Considering the treatment for adult ADHD is often the same stimulant drugs given to children, it should make one think about the implications of giving powerful amphetamines to people who may, in fact, have a substance abuse problem rather than ADHD!

campaigns mentioned above, many people arrive at the physician's office with self-diagnosed adult ADHD. In actuality, less than half of those who believe they have ADHD actually do, based on diagnostic criteria.[27] However, evaluating adults for an ADHD diagnosis without an "objective" standard (like the DSM-IV-TR in child ADHD) further complicates the problem. At least three assessment models exist for adult ADHD, though none are considered to be the "gold standard." From these three, Table 3 lists the symptoms and features that appear to be connected with adult ADHD while contrasting them with a limited Scriptural diagnosis and related Scriptural support.

Table 3

Adult ADHD Symptom	Scriptural Diagnosis(s)[28]	Scriptural Support
Childhood history of ADHD	Selfishness Lack of self control Impatience Rebellion Impulsiveness	Galatians 5:22-23 James 1:2-5; 5:7-11 I Peter 1:13-15; 2:19-23 Titus 2:11-12 2 Peter 1:5-6 Proverbs 17:11; 18:13,15; 25:28; 29: 11,20 Genesis 3:6-7 Hebrews 3:7-19 1 Samuel 15:22-25 Daniel 9:5-19 Joshua 24:14-15 Philippians 2:3-5 1 Corinthians 10:24 Romans 15:2-3 Matthew 20:26-28

---

[27] P. Roy-Byrne, L. Scheele, et.al. Adult attention-deficit hyperactivity disorder: assessment guidelines based on clinical presentation to a specialty clinic. Compr Psychiarty 1997;38:133-40

[28] Armand. P. Tiffe, *Transformed Into His Likeness: A Handbook for Putting Off Sin and Putting On Righteousness.* (Bemidji, MN.: Focus Publishing, 2005.

Hyperactivity and poor concentration	Disobedience Impatience Impulsiveness	1 Samuel 12:14-15; 15:22-25 Proverbs 13:13; 18:13 Matthew 7:24-27 John 14:15 James 1:2-5,22; 4:17; 5:7-11 Galatians 5:22-23 I Peter 1:13-15; 2:19-23 Titus 2:11-12 2 Peter 1:5-6 Proverbs 18:13,15; 25:28; 29:11,20 Genesis 3:6-7
At least two of the following: • Affective lability - rapid fluctuations in intensity and modality of emotions (euphoria to despair to anger, etc.) • Hot temper • Inability to complete tasks • Disorganization • Stress intolerance • Impulsivity	Lack of self-control, anger, selfishness, lack of perseverance, rebellion, defiance, impulsiveness	Proverbs 14:17,29; 15:18,32; 17:11; 18:13,15; 19:26; 25:28; 29:1,11,20; 30:17 Ephesians 4:31-32 Titus 2:11-12 James 1:5 I Peter 1:13-15; 2:19-23 2 Peter 1:5-6 Genesis 3:6-7 Hebrews 3:7-19 1 Samuel 15:22-25 Daniel 9:5-19 Joshua 24:14-15 Philippians 2:3-5 1 Corinthians 10:24 Romans 15:2-3 Matthew 20:26-28 Galatians 5:22-23 Deuteronomy 21:18-21 James 1:2-4; 5:7-11

Disinhibition – inability to restrain oneself from immediately responding; inability or difficulty monitoring one's own behavior	Lack of self-control Easily offended Rebellion Critical Fault finding Insensitivity	Matthew 7:1-2; 14:14; 15:32; 20:29-34; 22:39 Galatians 5:14-15, 22-23 Ephesians 4:2-3; Colossians 3:12 James 4:11-12 Proverbs 16:32; 19:11; 25:28 I Corinthians 13:5 I John 3:17; 3:8 Isaiah 58:6-12 Hebrews 3:7-19 Proverbs 17:11 1 Samuel 15:22-25 Daniel 9:5-19 Joshua 24:14-15 Titus 2:11-12 2 Peter 1:5-6
Adult ADHD Symptom	**Scriptural Diagnosis(s)**	**Scriptural Support**
Restlessness – difficulty relaxing or being chronically "on-edge"	Impatience Fear of man Worry	Matthew 6:25-34; 10:28-33; 26:69-75 Philippians 4:6-9 I Peter 2:19-23; 5:7 Psalm 37:5,25 Proverbs 29:25 Luke 12:4-5 John 12:42-43 Acts 5:29 Galatians 1:10; 5:22-23 1 Thessalonians 2:4-6 James 1:2-4; 5:7-11

Difficulty concentrating and paying attention – appointments and deadlines are frequently forgotten	Unworthy employee, uncontrolled thoughts, undependable, unreliable	Mark 7:21-23 Romans 12:2,11 2 Corinthians 10:4-5 Philippians 4:8 Matthew 5:37 Luke 12:41-47 1 Corinthians 4:2 Psalm 15 Ephesians 6:5-8 Colossians 3:22-25 1 Timothy 6:1-2 Titus 2:9-10 1 Peter 2:8
Socially inappropriate behavior – blurting out thoughts that are rude or insulting	Lack of self-control Argumentative Quarrelsome Careless talk Overly opinionated	Proverbs 10:19; 12:18; 15:1,28; 17:27-28; 18:2,13; 21:23; 25:28; 29:20 Matthew 5:9 Romans 12:18 Hebrews 12:14 James 1:19; 3:17-18 Psalm 19:14 Ephesians 4:29; 5:4 Colossians 4:6 James 1:26 Ecclesiastes 5:13 Galatians 5:22-23 Titus 2:11-12 2 Peter 1:5-6

Frustration over the inability to be organized	Self-pity Discontentment Self-sufficiency	Proverbs 15:16-17 Mark 4:7,18-19 Philippians 4:11-13 1 Timothy 6:6-8 Hebrews 6:11-20; 13:5 Psalm 42:1-11; 146:5 Romans 15:4,13 1 Corinthians 10:13 2 Corinthians 3:5; 4:7; 9:8 Ephesians 3:20 1 Peter 1:3,13 James 4:3-16 John 15:4-5 Luke 12:16-21 Daniel 4:29-37
Adult ADHD Symptom	**Scriptural Diagnosis(s)**	**Scriptural Support**
Trivial distractions receive inappropriate time and attention	Easily influenced to sin impulsiveness	Titus 2:11-12 James 1:5 I Peter 1:13-15 2 Peter 1:5-6 Proverbs 1:10; 18:13,15; 25:28; 29:11,20 Genesis 3:6-7 Daniel 1:8 Galatians 5:1 Ephesians 4:14; 6:10-18 Hebrews 4:14-16; 10:23 James 1:8; 4:17 1 Corinthians 10:13; 15:58
Difficulty initiating and organizing tasks	Selfishness Self-absorbed	Philippians 2:3-5 1 Corinthians 10:24 Romans 15:2-3 Matthew 20:26-28

Distractibility, daydreaming, memory difficulties	Foolishness and folly	Proverbs 1:7; 3:35; 10:1; 12:15; 14:3; 15:5; 16:20; 26:11-12
Drowsiness and inconsistent performance	Laziness Slothfulness	Proverbs 6:6-11; 10:4-5; 13:4; 14:23; 18:9; 24:30-34; 31:10-31 2 Thessalonians 3:7-12 1 Timothy 5:8
Difficulty managing criticism	Despising correction Easily offended Inadequate view of trials	Proverbs 3:11-12; 6:20-23; 12:1; 13:1; 15:5,12, 31-32; 16:32; 19:11; 22:15 1 Corinthians 13:5 2 Corinthians 4:16-18 Hebrews 12:1-3,5-11 James 1:2-4 1 Peter 1:6-7
Irritability and poor motivation	Anger Laziness Slothfulness	Proverbs 6:6-11; 10:4-5; 13:4; 14:17,23,29; 15:18; 18:9; 24:30-34; 25:28; 29:11; 31:10-31 Ephesians 4:31-32 1 Timothy 5:8 2 Thessalonians 3:7-12
Poor peer and family relationships	Unloving	Romans 12:9-10 Philippians 2:3-5 1 John 3:16-18; 4:7-10,20-21 Matthew 25:34-40
Learning problems and underachievement	Feelings of inferiority	Psalm 139:13-18 Jeremiah 31:3 Romans 5:8; 8:15-18 1 Corinthians 1:26-31 Ephesians 1:3-14 Philippians 4:13 1 Peter 1:18-19; 2:9-10 1 John 3:1

Unfortunately, the majority of these symptoms also are indicative of other "mental health" conditions thus a simple rating scale or cookbook approach is not adequate in making the diagnosis. The other conditions include major depression, bipolar disorder, generalized anxiety, substance abuse or dependence, personality disorders including borderline and antisocial varieties.[29] In addition, many of the same requirements exist for adults as with children in obtaining a clear diagnosis. A thorough history, including an interview with a spouse or parent is invaluable as is a thorough medical and family history. A comprehensive physical examination is also a must as are a battery of psychological and behavioral tests.

However, it goes without saying that each and every one of these thoughts, behaviors and feelings is addressed quite effectively by Scripture. Much of what is useful in children with ADHD is also applicable in adults and can be found throughout this book. Many of the other symptoms, seemingly unique to adults with ADHD, are addressed in the book of Proverbs alone (anger, rudeness, managing work and time, motivation, relationships, laziness, etc.) and can be applied as put off-put on's as described in chapters 3 and 11.

An accurate diagnosis is the key to solving problems. Medical issues should be dealt with by a competent medical professional. Problems of living or Spiritual problems should be dealt with using the Scriptures as applied by one who is mature enough to do so with discernment and wisdom. Medical issues should not be addressed Scripturally, (prayer notwithstanding) and Spiritual issues should not be dealt with medically. Discerning between the two, in order to arrive at a true diagnosis (instead of a Deceptive Diagnosis) is the challenge.

---

[29] R. Searight, J. Burke, F. Rottnek *Adult ADHD: Evaluation and Treatment in Family Medicine.* Am Fam Physician 2000;62:2077-86, 2091-2

Chapter 6
Case Study

While we realize case studies can seem artificial, they do serve a purpose in seeing how the counseling process flows. We believe the case below is a good example. It is abbreviated and much liberty is taken with respect to the responses of the counselees, however, it does provide some measure of practicality to the previous chapters. Poor little Archie has been much maligned throughout our book. Read the case below and see what the power of God's Word does for him.

Background information

Archie is an 8 year old boy, the second of three children. He has an older sister, Marsha, 11, who is a "straight A" student and a 5 year old younger brother, Peter. Because Archie attended a public school pre-school program, teachers were able to evaluate him before he started kindergarten. At age 6, he was assigned to a Cross-Category kindergarten classroom for children with learning or behavioral difficulties. Throughout the school year, Archie struggled to keep up with the other students in mathematics, writing and the alphabet. Thus, he repeated kindergarten at the insistence of school officials. They told his parents that Archie always seemed to be "elsewhere." He was said to be a "daydreamer" who, when pressed to perform, could do so, if he were interested. He was often found to be out of his seat, talking to others, or simply not paying attention.

Archie lives for recess time. He runs, jumps, climbs and is generally a carefree little boy. At home, he rides his bike, plays video games and plays in a city sponsored baseball league in the summer. Archie has never been in a fight and he is generally a respectful but very energetic child. His parents are active, working adults in their middle 30's. His father (Mike) is an architect and his mother (Carol) is an executive assistant at a financial services company. Both hold college degrees and are Christians. They regularly attend church. Both Archie and his older sister have made professions of faith while attending the church's AWANA program.

Throughout first grade, the school scheduled several parent-teacher conferences including a meeting with the school psychologist, putting pressure on Mike and Carol to have Archie evaluated for ADHD. Toward the end of his first grade year, Archie's parents were summoned to a "staffing" on Archie that was attended by the school principal, the school psychologist, Archie's teacher, and the school social worker. At the conclusion of the meeting, they were told Archie will need to be seen by the school's referral physician for a complete evaluation for ADHD before the beginning of the next school year.

Now Carol has come to you in tears, afraid of what is going to happen. She and Mike are opposed to medicating Archie as they do not see in Archie what the schools sees. Moreover, they are opposed to putting him on medications because of the effects they have seen on other children whose parents have acquiesced to the school's demands. As the church's Associate Pastor of Biblical Counseling and Discipleship, you agree to see them the following evening.

Counseling Session 1 – Mike and Carol only

Upon meeting Mike and Carol, you notice a professional looking couple with a genuine concern for their young son. After exchanging pleasantries, you get down to business by covering the *Consent to Counsel Document*[30] and discussing the questions they have about their role in the counseling process. You gather all of the information above as background. Thereafter, you explain the counseling process. You share with them your expectations, namely that they will be required to honor God, do what He says in His Word, and complete the homework assignments either individually or as a family. In turn, they can expect you to counsel them only from God's Word, not from psychology or some other system. As the counseling center is a ministry of the church, they will not have to pay fees for the counseling they receive. Lastly, you commit to counsel them God's way as long as it takes to deal with the issues presented, reassuring them that if they adhere to the expectations as presented, they can expect counseling last probably 6-10 sessions.

At this point, you ask several questions in order to get a better understanding of Archie and his entire family. As is the case with many families in this stage of life, controlled chaos is the norm. Mike is working long hours as he is attempting to make partner in his firm

---

[30] Consent to counsel documents have been published by several authors and counseling centers and are readily accessible via the internet.

and Carol is constantly busy taking one of the kids to any number of extracurricular activities. The family is rarely together and even more rarely shares a complete meal together. The children do not have any regular routine nor do they have a scheduled bedtime. Sunday's are the only day of the week where the family enjoys some semblance of "normalcy" as Mike and Carol have protected the day for the family.

Armed with this further information, you provide Mike and Carol with the great hope they have in Scripture, which is hope beyond hope. God has addressed these issues in Scripture and, through diligent effort on their part; they will be able to deal with the situation faithfully. Through I Corinthians 10:13, you assure them their problems are not unique and that God, in His faithfulness, has provided them with a way of escape so they can persevere through these trials[31]. Referencing Romans 8:28-29, you assure them that their circumstances are not accidental or due to bad luck. Though what they are experiencing with the school district is unpleasant, God will use it for their good in His perfect way. God has a plan for them, for their family and also for Archie and this is simply part of God's plan as He conforms them to the image of His Son Jesus Christ.[32]

You discuss how this applies to them and to Archie and you discuss the process going forward for helping Archie become more like Christ.

Mike and Carol's homework for the next session is to:
1. Complete the Personal Data Inventory data gathering tool[33]
2. Bring Archie to the next session.

---

[31] Giving hope to Archie and his parents is extremely important for successful counseling. For a detailed analysis of I Corinthians 10:13 and giving hope, see chapter six of Jay Adams' book *The Christian Counselor's Manual* (Zondervan) and *Christ and Your Problems* (P&R Publishing). See also Marshall Asher's book *The Armory: Equipment for Spiritual Warfare; Giving Hope* (Focus Publishing).

[32] For more information about counseling and the Sovereign work of God, see chapter two of Jay Adams' book *Competent to Counsel* (Zondervan), Marshall Asher's book *The Armory: Equipment for Spiritual Warfare; God's Sovereign Control* (Focus Publishing), and R.C. Sproul's book *The Invisible Hand* (P&R Publishing).

[33] The Personal Data Inventory is a data gathering instrument used by Biblical counselors. One example, may be found in Jay Adam's book *The Christian Counselors Manual* published by Zondervan Publishers.

Counseling Session 2 – Mike, Carol and Archie

Upon greeting everyone, you, in an abbreviated fashion, cover what occurred at the first session for Archie. Your explanations of Scripture are more descriptive and illustrative for his benefit. You collect the Personal Data Inventory and set it aside for future reference.

You talk with Archie about home and school and find that he likes school but that he has a hard time sitting still and following directions. He likes to talk to his friends and he does not enjoy being cooped up all day. There are about 30 children in his classroom and he likes his teacher, though he says she is sometimes boring. You ask all of them to discuss a "typical" school day. Mike is up and out of the house by 7:00 am. Carol is responsible for getting Marsha, Archie and Peter ready for school. Marsha and Archie are essentially on their own for breakfast and Archie takes advantage of Mom's absence by consuming cookies, pastries, donuts or other sugary treats along with fruit juice or soda-pop.

After school, all the children attend a latch-key program and Carol picks them up after work. Upon arriving at home, the kids all have a "self-guided" snack. Marsha often reads or does homework while Archie and Peter play baseball or video games together. Marsha has piano lessons two afternoons per week and attends a weekly Girl Scout meeting. Archie and Peter play soccer in the spring and fall and take swimming lessons over the winter. Archie is in Boy Scouts and Peter is in Cub Scouts and they have a den meeting each month during school and each week over the summer. Also over the summer, Archie has baseball games or practices three evenings per week, and Peter has T-ball games two evenings per week. When school is out for the summer, Carol's mother watches the kids throughout the day.

As the entire picture of the family begins to come together, you begin to have a discussion of habit. Why is it we do the things we do? (For a detailed discussion see chapters 3 and 11). Much of Archie's behavior is due, in part, to a lack of self-control and self-discipline and a focus on self in general. Archie needs to put off the old way of life, renew his mind through Scripture, and put on the new. As a Christian, Archie is to be conformed to the likeness of Christ, and in order to do so he will need to exchange those thoughts and behaviors that are unrighteous with those that are righteous. This is accomplished in and through immersion in the Word so that righteous habits are replacing unrighteous habits.

Change always begins with repentance. Archie needs to repent of the sin of not paying attention and seek forgiveness from God and neighbor. However, repentance is not an end of itself, but a beginning. Repentance must lead to change or putting off and putting on of behavior. Archie needs to put off the old habit of not paying attention and put on the biblical alternative habit of paying attention. The put off and put on assigned to Archie to memorize is Luke 2:46. *"Then, after three days they found Him in the temple, sitting in the midst of the teachers, both listening to them and asking them questions."* The put off, not paying attention or listening, is implied (See chapters 3 and 11).

Using his computer, Archie is instructed to type "Put off" and then write "not paying attention" and "not listening". Below the "Put off" Archie is to type "Put on" and then type out the entire verse Luke 2:24 blowing up the font so it fills the entire page. He is instructed not to simply hide his put off and put on verse in his heart (Psalm 119:11), but to make copies and post one in his room, bathroom, in the living room, over the television set, on the refrigerator, on the back door and on the front door. These are referred to as "stop signs." In addition his parents, two or three times each day, need to ask him, "Archie, what's your put off and put on?" Even when he says it perfectly they should continue to ask him to recite it. A person can memorize a verse and not think about it. Do you, the reader, know John 3:16 by heart? Have you thought of John 3:16 today? You want Archie to think of his verse dozens of times a day.

The following week, Archie and his siblings are registered to attend your church's Vacation Bible School (VBS) so you encourage him to practice his put off and put on verse. Since there will be no put off and put on verses posted at Vacation Bible School, it will be helpful for Archie to tie a string on his finger or put a rubber band loosely around his wrist. Whenever Archie sees or feels the string or rubber band it will remind him of his put off and put on verse.

Remember, habits are learned ways of living. Archie practiced "not paying attention" until it became a part of him. In the same way righteous habits are acquired through practice. The secret to godliness is discipline (I Timothy 4:7). You, Mike and Carol must help Archie discipline himself for the purpose of godliness. Discipline means work. It means daily effort. It means self-denial (Matthew 16:24).

Archie's homework after this session includes:

1. Repent to God and neighbor for not paying attention.

2. Memorize, Luke 2:46, your put off and put on verse.

3. Post your stop signs (an example of Archie's stop sign follows) around the house as mentioned previously.

4. When Archie attends VBS tie a string or place a rubber band around your wrist to remind you of your put on and put on verse.

Mike and Carol's homework is to:

1. Ask Archie to recite his put off and put on verse three to four times each day. Make a large sign on 8.5 x 11 paper:

PUT OFF
Not Paying Attention
Not Listening

PUT ON

"Then, after three days they found Him in the temple, sitting in the midst of the teachers, both listening to them and asking them questions" (Luke 2:46).

Counseling Session Three – Mike, Carol, and Archie

You follow up on all homework assigned in session #2 and ask Archie if he has memorized his put off and put on verse (Luke 2:46) and posted it around the house. Archie says he knows the verse however, when you ask him to recite it he stumbles in a couple of places. You explain that Archie needed to hide the verse in his heart as Psalm 119:11 says to do. You then asked him if he knows John 3:16. Archie smiles and without hesitation recites John 3:16 perfectly. You praise him and say "that's what it means to hide your put off and put on verse in your heart. You know it like you know John 3:16."

Having observed the family and gathered data from them both through the previous two counseling sessions as well as through the PDI, you ask them to turn in Scripture and read Matthew 5:29-30 and a similar passage in Matthew 18:8-9:

> **"If your right eye makes you stumble, tear it out and throw it from you; for it is better for you to lose one of the parts of your body, than for your whole body to be thrown into hell. If your right hand makes you stumble, cut it off and throw it from you; for it is better for you to lose one of the parts of your body, than for your whole body to go into hell"** (Matthew 5:29-30).

> **"If your hand or your foot causes you to stumble, cut it off and throw it from you; it is better for you to enter life crippled or lame, than to have two hands or two feet and be cast into the eternal fire. If your eye causes you to stumble, pluck it out and throw it from you. It is better for you to enter life with one eye, than to have two eyes and be cast into the fiery hell"** (Matthew 18:8-9).

You explain that in these passages, Jesus in not teaching that we should practice self-mutilation. The body is not what causes us to sin as the Gnostics taught, rather sin flows from the heart. Removing part of the body will not prevent us from sinning. What Jesus is teaching here is what biblical counselors refer to as "radical amputation." Part of putting off the old habits sometimes may involve incapacitating oneself so that it is hard to sin in the same way. Radical amputation recognizes the fact that Archie will repeat his sin, as he has in the past, and prepares him for the temptation. It is the means which Archie

73

takes action to prevent him from repeating his sinful behavior. Jay Adams said, "The passage in Matthew 5 directs him to take definitive, concrete, radical action. The offending member—eye, hand, foot; it doesn't matter—must be removed so that it no longer can be used to commit the sin in question: that is radical amputation."[34]

As the family begins to understand your teaching, you take the opportunity to point out some things in their lives which may need to be dealt with in this manner. First, Archie will need to "amputate" the sugary breakfast in favor of something more balanced. Some more balanced options include granola and milk, scrambled egg(s) and toast, a boiled egg and a muffin, waffles and ham, oatmeal with raisins and nuts, or pancakes with flavored yogurt. The key is to achieve a balance between carbohydrates (sugars), protein and fat. The same principle should be applied as well to his afternoon snack. Archie may also need to have the amount of time he plays video games "amputated" as well, at least until his homework and chores are completed and until after the family has dinner together. Both of these activities (unbalanced breakfast and excessive video games) may be leading Archie to behave inconsistently with the teaching of Luke 2:46, thus they should be dealt with immediately.

In addition, some semblance of order and structure needs to be introduced into the home environment. You remind Mike and Carol of the biblical order of things as being God first, spouse second, children third, and everything else thereafter. Having the children involved in every imaginable activity does not achieve what it is often intended to achieve. Remember the exhortation on Psalm 46:10:

> **"Be still, and know that I am God. I will be exalted among the nations; I will be exalted in the earth!"**
> (ESV) (Emphasis ours)

The family is caught up in considerable "peripheral" activities and they have become blinded by their busyness. This busyness and lack of structure may very well be contributing to Archie's problem behavior and it will likely lead to other difficulties as well.

As for homework, based on your observations and teaching, you talk with Archie about how his behavior can affect other people, not just himself. Not paying attention, interrupting others when they are speaking, getting out of his seat are all examples of self-focused behavior. Archie does not want to listen to his teacher; he wants to stare out the window and daydream or play with his pencil. Even

---

[34] Jay Adams, *A Theology of Christian Counseling* (Grand Rapids, MI.: Zondervan Publishing House, 1979), p.265.

though the teacher has called upon another student to speak, Archie, because he is self-focused, interrupts. He often feels what he has to say is more important. Archie desires to do what he wants to do and not what he is instructed to do by his teacher. Archie puts himself before others. He is behaving selfishly.

The counselor assigns a second put-off and put-on verse for selfishness.

Philippians 2:3 is intended to remind Archie to always consider others ahead of himself. It reads:

> **"Do nothing from selfishness or empty conceit, but with humility of mind regard one another as more important than yourselves..."**

Archie must put off selfishness and put on humility. Humility is regarding "another as more important than yourselves." Instead of focusing on himself, Archie must get into the habit of putting his neighbor first. As Archie practices righteous behavior, he will become habituated to it, putting off the unrighteous behavior at the same time.

You encourage Mike and Carol to take a serious look at their priorities in life and make radical amputations. You remind them of the seriousness of the issue with Archie and the warning they had received from the school officials. There is much at stake and there is much to gain. God will bless the decisions they make if they are faithful to the teachings of Scripture. You remind them again of Romans 8:28 and that while all things may not be good in themselves, God is using ALL things for His glory and for their benefit. Like I Corinthians 10:13, He is providing a way of escape in being obedient to His Word. You close in earnest prayer for the family and the work they need to be undertaking.

Archie's homework for session three is:
1. Repent before God and neighbor of your selfishness and ask Him and them for forgiveness.
2. Continue working on his put-off and put-on for paying attention, Luke 2:46
3. Memorize and make stop signs for the additional put-off and put-on for selfish behavior, Philippians 2:3
4. Practice humility by performing three acts of love[35] every

---
[35] An act of love is something he may not normally do, but when he begins to think

day. Write down the acts of love and bring them to the next session.

Homework for Mike and Carol includes:
1. Two to three times each day, ask Archie to recite his put-off and put-on verses.
2. Amputate the sugary breakfast in favor of something more balanced. Record Archie's daily menu choices and bring them to the next session.
3. Write down two to three things they need to amputate that would add more order and structure to the home environment. Do those things. Bring the list to the next session.

Counseling Session 4 – Mike, Carol and Archie

At the beginning of session 4, you collect and review all homework assignments. Once again, Archie is asked to recite his put-off and put-on verses and he does so perfectly. He has posted the stop signs as instructed by the counselor. He has his list of acts of love that he has performed and you review his list. Mike and Carol are pleased by the way God has worked in Archie's life as a result of his obedience to God's word. They tell you Archie is doing much better at home and at Bible school. You encourage them that even though things are better, they should not slack off. Improvements do not necessarily mean put-off and put-on has occurred. You further explain that, as when taking an antibiotic for an infection, while you may feel better after three or four days, it is imperative to take the medication for the full duration of the prescription. Failing to do so may cause the infection to become resistant to the medication which makes further treatment more difficult. Likewise, failing to be diligent in the put-off and put-on process for the entire 5-7 weeks can lead to failure to permanently change. Subsequent attempts then become progressively more difficult.

You follow up on Mike and Carol's homework assignments as well. They tell you that they have faithfully asked Archie several times

---

of others ahead of himself, performing acts of love for others emphasizes the point. He may consider picking up his room without being told, gathering his dirty clothes and taking them to the laundry room, clearing the dinner table, paying attention to the VBS teacher when she is reading the Bible story, waiting in line patiently as the class gathers for their snacks, or a host of other acts similar to these. The point is to put others before himself as an illustration of Christlikeness.

each day to recite his verses. You inquire about their assignment to amputate Archie's sugary breakfast, reminding them how a diet high in sugars may impede Archie's progress. Carol states she has been much more organized in the mornings and is taking a more active role in helping all the children choose a balanced breakfast. She took your earlier recommendations with respect to food choices, has amputated the sugary foods and has replaced them with the menu items you suggested in the previous session.

You are pleased and encourage the family to continue in their efforts to change.

Homework for Archie is to:

1. Continue working on his put-off and put-on for paying attention, Luke 2:46

2. Continue working on his put-off and put-on for selfish behavior, Philippians 2:3

3. Practice humility by performing three acts of love every day. Write down the acts of love and bring them to the next session.

You ask Mike and Carol to very seriously consider additional activities to be amputated in order to add even more structure and organization to their home life. They have made some changes and others are necessary. You remind them, rather directly, of the Biblical order of life being God first, spouse second, children third and everything else thereafter, while referring back to the scriptures on radical amputation.

Homework for Mike and Carol includes:

1. Studying Ephesians 5 and 6 regarding the biblical order of life

2. Review of the teaching on radical amputation from the previous session

You schedule your next session for two weeks later rather than one due to a planned vacation with your own family.

Session 5 – Mike, Carol, and Archie (2 weeks from the previous appointment)

At the beginning of session five, you collect all the homework from the previous session and turn your attention to Archie. He quotes his verses flawlessly and quickly lists off his three acts of love for each of the two weeks. Knowing you gave Mike and Carol the difficult assignment, you ask what God had shown them in Ephesians 5 and 6 and Matthew 5 and 18.

Mike interjects that he has some exciting news. He tells you that he and Carol were numb after the last counseling session. At first, they felt shame and guilt for letting their family get so out of hand. It was nearly a sleepless night for both of them. Mike said he first became angry and then, as he thought and prayed about it more, he saw where he had fallen short. He was putting his career ahead of his wife and children. What he thought was investing in their future was actually undercutting their present and seriously impacting the future he so desperately wanted to secure. Carol shared that she was so caught up in having the kids involved with all the "right" activities that she had neglected Mike and, at times, the children themselves. They studied the passages you shared and looked up their meaning in a couple of online commentaries to learn more and they both confessed their own personal relationship with God had fallen way down on their priority list. After a couple more days of discussion, prayer, contemplation, conviction and repentance, they had made some decisions.

First, Carol had spoken with her company about moving into a part-time position. She would transition to a six-hour work day, working 9:00am to 3:00pm, and move to another department. This change would allow her to get the kids off to school calmly, including managing their breakfasts, while leaving her plenty of time to get to work. Mike, on the other hand, met with the managing partners of his firm and informed them he was going to be making some changes in his work practices. He realized and they agreed that it would take him longer to make partner, but that his marriage and family would have to come first. Furthermore, Mike and Carol had spoken individually with each of their children about what activities could go and which ones they wanted to continue. They were surprised to learn that the kids actually welcomed the less hectic schedule and more time spent together.

Mike states he has already transitioned to a strict 40-hour work week. This has allowed him to arrive at home in time to assist Carol in the preparation of the evening meal and has allowed the entire family time to come together on a regular daily basis around the dinner table. Here, they have been able to discuss the events of the day. Even in the short time since making the change, Mike has already noticed how much more he is becoming connected and involved with both Carol and each one of the children. When school starts back up in the fall, Mike shares his desire to begin a family devotion time one evening per week and a regular "date-night" with Carol.

Carol states that she too has made the transition to the new department and the new hours. With the added time each day, she is beginning to more effectively manage the household. Carol is embracing her role as the manger of the home and has enjoyed much less anxiety and worry about getting things done as they should be. She has instituted regular chores for each of the children, and has more time to spend with them in the mornings and afternoons. Her evenings are freer to enjoy time with Mike. She too is looking forward to school starting in the fall. Carol is excited about having time to get the children off to school each morning and being there in the afternoons to pick them up and help them with homework.

Summary of Sessions 6-8 – Mike, Carol and Archie

The remaining sessions consist of follow-up, reinforcement, and encouragement that putting-off and putting-on takes time (5-7 weeks). God's goal for Archie is to be complete in Christ. We see this in Colossians 1:28 where Paul teaches:

> **We proclaim Him, admonishing every man and teaching every man with all wisdom, so that we may present every man complete in Christ**.

Other ways of saying the same thing include being *"conformed to the image of His Son"* (Romans 8:29), being more like Jesus, growing in the Lord, or becoming more Christ-like. In Colossians 1:29, Paul very practically instructs us on how to actually be complete. He says, *"For this purpose also I labor, striving according to His power, which mightily works within me."* He says two things here, Archie must labor and strive. For example, Archie is coming to counseling, memorizing his verses, posting his stop signs and doing his acts of love. However, since all behaviors are heart or spiritual issues, all the laboring and striving in the world (works) will not please God. The goal is NOT behavioral modification. The Pharisees of Jesus time were behavior modificationists as they prayed, tithed and followed the law. Jesus said they were hypocrites because their hearts were far from Him (Matthew 6). The goal of biblical counseling is much higher. It strives to effect change of the heart. True heart change can only be accomplished by God.

Secondly, this striving and laboring is according to God's word.[36] It understands the biblical dynamic of habit and change as taught in Scripture. Moreover, in concert with Archie's laboring and striving, God's power works mightily IN Archie to bring about change. Thus, Archie must work AND God must work. It is not an either/or proposition. Both human effort and Divine intervention are required to realize true change. Change, therefore, is a spiritual activity since all behavior flows from the heart. Heart change in becoming more like Christ is similar to the process that occurs when one is saved. For example, you believed according to the Word and the Holy Spirit brings about the second birth or salvation. With Archie, he has to confidently work (labor and strive) by faith, knowing that as a result of his obedience the Holy Spirit will effect heart change. This is the primary reason biblical counseling is not effective for the unregenerate man. Unbelievers are sensitive only to the Gospel call of salvation. All other reasoning from scripture is foolishness to them (Colossians 1:18, I Corinthians 2:14).

Epilogue

Throughout this case study, our focus has been primarily on Archie. We have deliberately ignored potentially numerous other problems that are likely present. In reality, there would likely be significant other issues involving other family members. For example, there are commonly marital problems that need to be addressed in addition to those mentioned. Mike and Carol may be experiencing unrighteous anger toward each other, toward Archie, toward the school officials, or even toward God. In addition, there may be a plethora of other complicating problems affecting the family dynamic. In these cases, separate counseling may be necessary for Mike and Carol alone or with the other children.

---

[36] The Bible is filled with admonitions calling on believers to make an effort to change. A few examples for further reference regarding how man is admonished to put forth that effort include Ephesians 4:25, 31; Philippians 2:3; I Corinthians 6:18; Psalm 37:1a.

Chapter 7
ADHD: Psychiatry and Psychology Go To School

To fully understand how psychology and psychiatry have caused ADHD and many of the other "syndromes" and "disorders" which our children today supposedly suffer from, it is necessary to take note of the influence they have had on the thought of Western society—especially on child education.

> **Jan Strydom & Susan du Plessis**
> *The Myth of ADHD and Other Learning Disabilities*

Children's behavior is increasingly portrayed through a psychological label. They are often diagnosed as depressed or traumatized. And while there is still a debate about the validity of the diagnosis of school phobia, virtually any energetic or disruptive child could acquire the label of 'attention deficit hyperactive disorder'.

> **Frank Furedi,** *Therapy Culture*

In Greek Mythology, Sirens were part human, part bird. They lived on a rocky island in the middle of the sea where they sang their beautiful songs. Sailors, spellbound by the enchanting melodies, would jump into the water or steer their ships toward the island. Either way, the Sirens of Greek legend lured sailors off course to their destruction on the rocks.

The Song of the Siren is reminiscent of how over the past thirty years, through an unrelenting public relations campaign, through many in the medical community, and through countless books on the subject, millions of parents and teachers have been enchanted into believing in the existence of a psychiatric illness called "attention deficit disorder."

They attend the conferences, read the books, and listen to the tapes of behavioral experts and are mesmerized by the call and lulled into thinking "A.D.D. must be a real disease."

Children who were once considered to be "full of energy," "quick to respond" or "daydreamers" are now diseased and abnormal. They have the three classic ADHD symptoms; they are hyperactive, distractible, and impulsive. Years ago they were thought of as being normal children who needed to "get their energy out," or "blow off a little steam." Today their medication is carefully measured out and managed to control "dysfunctional" behavior.

While its advocates claim it to be a brain disease, its opponents, many of which are world renowned psychologists such as David B. Stein, Ph.D., psychiatrists such as Peter R. Breggin, M.D., and neurologists such as Fred A. Baughman, M.D., are denying its very existence. In his book, *Unraveling the ADD/ADHD Fiasco* David B. Stein wrote:

> Even during my years of training, psychologists and psychiatrists tried to convince both the professional community and the public that inattention and overactive children had a disease. This means that something is terribly wrong with their brain or nervous system that causes their inattention and misbehavior. There was not a shred of evidence to support such a claim.[37]

In his book, *Toxic Psychiatry*, Peter Breggin wrote:

> Hyperactivity is the most frequent justification for drugging children. The difficult-to-control male is certainly not a new phenomenon, but attempts to give him a medical diagnosis are the product of modern psychology and psychiatry. At first psychiatrists called hyperactivity a brain disease. When no brain disease could be found, they changed it to "minimal brain disease (MBD). When no minimal brain disease could be found the profession transformed the concept into "minimal brain dysfunction." When no minimal brain dysfunction could be demonstrated, the label became attention deficit disorder. Now it's just assumed to be a real disease, regardless of the failure to prove it so.

---

[37] John K. Rosemond, David B. Stein's *Unraveling The ADD/ADHD Fiasco*, (Kansas City, MO: Andrew McMeel Books, 2001), Forward.

> Biochemical imbalance is the code word, but there's no
> more evidence for that than there is for actual brain
> disease.[38]

Fred Baughman wrote:

> ADHD is not a disorder or a disease or a syndrome
> or a chemical imbalance of the brain, it is not over-
> diagnosed or under-diagnosed or misdiagnosed. It
> does not exist in 3% or 5% or 15% of the population. It
> is a 100% fraud.[39]

The history of attention deficit hyperactive disorder is not like the stories of how other diseases such as polio, diabetes, or AIDS were discovered. It was not revealed by scientists in a world renowned research hospital who, through years of painstaking research, uncovered a hidden disease that had been waiting for decades to be discovered. ADHD was voted into existence in 1987 by a committee of the American Psychiatric Association. The recognition of ADHD as a "psychiatric disorder" was the culmination of social, political, economic, medical, and psychological factors coming together at just the right time. Bolstered by politics and money, the outrageous claims of the ADHD industry have persistently escaped scrutiny. As a result, millions of responsible and loving parents have medicated their children on the advice of the "experts" in child behavior. Additionally, as an outgrowth of the wildly successful ADHD drug industry, today there are pharmacological treatments for adults who are unable to concentrate.

Drapetomania: A Disease Called Freedom

"Drapetomania" was a psychiatric diagnosis in 1851. It was made by a Louisiana surgeon, psychologist and American Medical Association member, Samuel A. Cartwright. By combining the Greek words *drapeto*, to flee, and *mania*, craze, Cartwright explained the tendency of black slaves to flee captivity was caused by a disease. Slave owners, who felt they were improving the lives of their slaves, could not understand why they desired to escape. The diagnosis appeared in the *New Orleans Medical and Surgical Journal*, where Dr.

---

[38] Peter Breggin, *Toxic Psychiatry*, (New York, NY: St. Martin's Press, 1991), p.278.

[39] Fred A. Baughman, Jr. and Craig Hovey, *The ADHD Fraud*, (Victoria, BC: Trafford Publishing, 2006), p.9.

Cartwright argued that it was in fact a treatable medical disorder. Slaves showing early signs of drapetomania, reflected in moody, resentful, sullen and dissatisfied behavior, should be whipped strictly as an early intervention. Whipping was to be utilized as a primary intervention once the "disease" had progressed to the stage of actually running away.

Disease is everywhere. Disease afflicts humans, animals and plants. It is spoken of in everyday conversation. Newspapers and magazines are filled with articles on disease. Congress enacts legislation regarding disease. The subject of disease is the topic of books. Physicians seek to combat disease. Insurance companies offer reimbursement for those treated for disease. Philosophers debate disease. Dictionaries and encyclopedias define disease. Disease, like the sword of Damocles, hangs heavy over the human consciousness.

The word disease is as commonly used in everyday conversation as the words television, foot or rake. To complain that one's foot hurts requires no further explanation as to the meaning of the word foot. The word is understood and obvious to all. The consensus we have regarding so many commonly used terms creates an assumption that the meaning of disease is equally obvious to all. No further explanation or analysis is necessary. Since disease is such a part of our everyday life one might presume we all know exactly what is meant by the word disease, but that is not the case. Ivan Illich wrote, "Each civilization defines its own diseases." What some may consider being a disease (drapetomania, kleptomania, alcoholism, etc.), others may call freedom, crime, or sin. For the same symptom of habitual stealing, a person may be executed, have their hand cut off, be imprisoned, be forced into mandatory therapy or be hospitalized depending upon the country in which they steal.

Diseases and disorders may differ from country to country or one generation to the next. What is considered normal in the United States may be considered abnormal in Thailand. What one generation considers being normal another generation considers abnormal. In 1952 the American Psychiatric Association published the *Diagnostic and Statistical Manual for Mental Disorders* (DSM). One hundred and twelve mental disorders were defined of which homosexuality was included. In 1980, DSM-III was published and homosexuality was removed from the manual. The decision was not based on new advances and discoveries in science. Precipitated by active lobbying from the homosexual community, the American Psychiatric Association convened and voted. By a margin of 5,854 to 3,810 homosexuality, a long-standing form of abnormal behavior became a scientifically-declared form of "sexual preference." Conversely, many behaviors which were considered normal twenty years ago have been added to the DSM and defined as syndromes, disorders, disabilities, and diseases. If your child does poorly in math he may have number 315.4, *Developmental Arithmetic Disorder*. If your son is argumentative and disobedient he may need medication for number 313.8, *Oppositional Defiant Disorder*. If your child has trouble reading he probably has number 315.00, *Reading Disorder*. If his writing skills fall below what is expected of him, call a psychologist immediately as he may have number 315.2 *Disorder of Written Expression*. If your child has problems learning, but does not meet the criteria of any specific Learning Disorder then it may be more serious than you think. He may be suffering from number 315.9 *Learning Disorder Not Otherwise Specified*. Remember, disorder connotes disease. From the first publication of the DSM in 1952 to the present DSM-IV edition, the number of mental diseases has increased from 112 to today's grand total of 374. And that number will undoubtedly grow with the next new version of the DSM.

The Brief History of ADHD

One of the first secular references to a hyperactive child seems to have been in the poem, *Fidgety Phil*, written by German physician Heinrich Hoffman in 1865.

Fidgety Phil,

He won't sit still,

He wriggles,

And giggles,

And then, I declare,

Swings backwards and forwards

And tilts in his chair…

The medicalization of attention deficit hyperactive disorder seems to have taken place in 1902. George Still, an English pediatrician, theorized the problem with children who were "bundles of energy, daydreamers" and highly misbehaving had something wrong with their brain. In a series of lectures to the Royal College of Physicians, Still described 20 children in his clinical practice who he defined as having a deficit in "volitional inhibition." Lawlessness, spitefulness, cruelty, and dishonestly was also characteristic of these children. The "keynote" quality in these children, Still proposed, was the immediate gratification of the self. In light of the adequate rearing these children received, he speculated there may be a biological cause to their unrestrained behavior. Learning many members of these children's families had "psychiatric illnesses," Still theorized that there must be a genetically inherited proneness toward moral corruption. Genetics and biology, he concluded, as opposed to free will, should be considered in assessing these children.

Still's new way of thinking would have far reaching implications in our times. Previously, "bad" and uncontrolled behavior was seen as a moral failing or sin. The parents or child or both were held responsible. Physical punishment was the "treatment." Books of that time instructed parents how to correctly spank their child. As psychiatry and psychology began to infer that neurology, rather than a sinful heart, was the cause of deviant behavior, a different approach to child-rearing emerged. Unfortunately, even though no objective evidence existed, the disease theory for ADHD had its foundation.

The biological theory of sinful behaviors, the precursor of ADHD, received a big boost in North America with an outbreak of an encephalitis epidemic which affected large numbers of children in 1917 – 1918. Physicians noticed children who survived this brain infection often developed symptoms such as impaired memory, inattention, hyperactivity, irritability, etc. It was the conclusion of Dr. F. G. Ebaugh that perhaps another virus or the encephalitis virus itself caused damage to the brain resulting in the bad behavior (Postencephalitic Behavior Disorder). Again, it was only a guess. There was no proof; however, it fueled support for the disease model of behavior and the concept of brain-injured child syndrome. Brain damage would come to be applied to children manifesting the same behavioral features of children who had encephalitis, but without evidence of brain damage. In other words, children who behave in the same way as brain damaged children, it was erroneously deduced, must have brain damage. It is the same argument as "dogs have tails, therefore, every animal with a tail must be a dog." The logic is faulty.

During the 1920s and 1930s other researchers investigated the relationship between behavior problems in children and birth trauma or post-birth head injuries. In 1937, the first use of psychoactive drugs to control hyperactivity was introduced by Dr. Charles Bradley. Bradley observed that by using Benzedrine™ (amphetamine), a stimulant, the unwanted behavior of these highly active and inattentive children was suppressed. Bradley could not explain how a stimulant helped a hyperactive child become less stimulated. He could only report that it worked and it became known as the "paradoxical effect." The paradoxical effect remained popular for many years and was said to be proof that hyperactivity and inattention was a disease. This way of thinking is known as allopathic logic and it runs rampant in the mental heath field. If a drug "works," then there must be a "disease." It is also known as pragmatism. Many parents we have counseled still believe it today. However, in 1988 it was discovered that stimulants have the same effect on all people as they do on those labeled ADHD. More recently, college health care centers are reporting a growing trend among students to turn to prescription stimulants like Adderall® and Ritalin® when cramming for exams. Students "claim they can study for eight hours straight, write 30-page papers in one sitting, and somehow become engrossed in lectures they ordinarily find boring."[40] A study in the *Journal of American College Health* in 2005 found that "17 percent of men and 11 percent of women at a Midwestern university said they illegally used drugs intended for people with ADHD. As for who uses the drugs and when, 'it's mostly during major study periods, and for people who don't have the attention span.'"[41]

The name for kids on the go, moving, climbing and not paying attention has changed many times over the past 100 years. However, in 1940 researchers studying the effects of brain damage injury observed distractibility and hyperactivity in mentally retarded children. The study was published in 1947 under the title *Psychopathology and Education of the Brain-Injured Child*. This work laid the foundation for the terms "minimal brain damage" (MBD), and "minimal brain dysfunction" (MBD) used in the 1950s and 1960s. However, when no evidence was produced to demonstrate brain damage existed, these terms fell out of favor. The term "hyperkinetic reaction of childhood" was settled on by the American Psychological Association in 1968 and published in the *Diagnostic and Statistical Manuel of Mental Disorders, Second Edition* (DSM-II).

---

[40] *Belleville News Democrat* (Belleville, Illinois), August 13, 2006
[41] *Ibid.*

In the 1970s the focus of research was on attention problems. Deficits in attention were thought to be the real culprit according to Canadian researcher Virginia Douglas, M.D. By this time hundreds of thousands of children had been diagnosed with some variant of this problem and were being treated with drugs. There was no consensus as to causal factors and diagnostic criteria. The only consensus was stimulant drugs, such as methylphenidate (Ritalin® Concerta® Metadate® and others), were the therapy. If a child responded well to the medication, as previously stated, he had the disease.

The claim that ADHD is a disease must be substantiated by an objective anatomical or physiologic abnormality (abnormality = disease; no abnormality = normal = no disease). Over the years, countless possible biological causes have been proposed including genetic factors, chemical imbalances, diet, television, video games, food additives, etc. In 1990, in search of a physical cause, Alan Zametkin, M.D. and his colleagues at the National Institute of Mental Health published a study in the prestigious *New England Journal of Medicine*. The article appeared to link hyperactivity in adults with reduced metabolism of glucose (this would mean an over abundance of glucose, a prime source of energy, resulting in hyperactivity) in areas of the brain involved in the control of attention, planning and motor activity. Proponents of ADHD and the media quickly reported "proof" of a medical basis for ADHD had been discovered. Parents of children with ADHD heaved a sigh of relief that bratty kids and / or poor parenting were not the culprit. Three years later in the *Archives of General Psychiatry* the efforts of Zametkin and others to repeat the 1990 study found no significant differences between the brains of so-called hyperactive subjects and those of so-called normal subjects. In other words, they could not substantiate their earlier findings. Nevertheless, references to ADHD as a "neurobiological disorder," based on Zametkin's 1990 study, appear throughout CHADD's (Children and Adults with Attention Deficit Disorder) literature. They do not mention the follow-up studies that failed to confirm the original findings.

Similarly, in another critique of Zametkin's research, members of the University of Nebraska indicated that Zametkin did not clarify whether the lower glucose rates found in "hyperactive brains" were a *cause* or a *result* of attention problems. There are many known causes of attention problems like problems at home, a boring teacher, or lead or pesticide poisoning. The critics pointed out that if levels of epinephrine (adrenaline) were monitored, shortly following a person being startled, one would not say the person has an epinephrine (adrenaline) disorder. Instead, the underlying conditions that led to abnormal epinephrine (adrenaline) levels would be examined.

In spite of the fact there is no proof that ADHD has a medical cause, like drapetomania, the theory has, through repeating it over and over, taken on the cultural authority of proven fact.

Disorderly Education

No one heard of it before 1965. It went from virtual anonymity to epidemic proportions, by the mid 1970s. It has been known by many different names and is associated, oftentimes synonymously with minimal brain dysfunction, hyperkinesis, and others. There are no universally accepted symptoms. There are no perceptible anatomical or biochemical distinctives which make a diagnosis possible. It is said to afflict as many as 40 per cent of all American children and the cause of most learning and behavioral problems. It has united a flotilla of physicians, mental health and educational professionals and drug companies in undoubtedly the most zealous and powerful movement in contemporary education. Its most common name is "learning disabilities."

Learning disabilities (LD) are purported to be the cause of nearly all school failures and juvenile delinquency. Nearly every other social affliction in our time can be traced in part to learning disabilities. Consequently, a growing number of states began promoting screening of school children for learning disabilities. Inservice training for teachers was mandated in remediation techniques. Some were trained and certified as LD specialists. The Association for Children with Learning Disabilities (ACLD) and the American Foundation for Learning Disabilities held conventions and launched public information campaigns. A retrieval system was based at the Massachusetts Institute of Technology where the public could access quick information about LD evaluation centers, programs and professionals in their area. A massive movement was underway as indicated by the growing number of and membership in learning disability organizations. From 1965 – 1975 the nation went from no LD training programs in colleges and universities, no inservice training, no summer workshops to literally hundreds of these programs. In the mid-1960s only an insignificant number of children were taking medication for LD or hyperkinesis. Today millions of preschoolers and school age children are taking psychoactive drugs dispensed by local schools to treat their hyperkinesis or ADHD.

Hyperkinesis became the most common of the "learning disabilities." There is nothing new about parents and teachers complaining that children are difficult to teach and control. What is new is childhood behaviors being attributed to brain abnormalities. Children, who were lazy, rebellious, non-compliant, etc., prior to World War I, were regarded as defective in will and moral character. If they did study hard, but still exhibited difficulty in school work, they were considered slow learners. In the 1950's, Sigmund Freud and psychoanalysis became fashionable in education. Failure was attributed to "emotional problems or handicaps" or overbearing parents. In the 1960's, failure was attributed to "cultural disadvantages" and discrimination. By the mid-1960's, failure of particular groups of children, primarily those who were poor or black, led to a movement to reform education. The plan targeted every conceivable minority. The education system, not the individual, would be the focus of remediation. However, by the 1970's, the social mood changed, tax increases were voted down, federal money dried up and it was all over. Whereas relevant curriculum and better teachers were once demanded, the complaint was now focused on school violence. Communities exerted more and more pressure on school boards and administrators to tighten the budget, control the kids and teach the basics. However, traditional education had already been discredited in the previous decade and the search was on for something more scientific and modern. The "early intervention" concepts popularized by Head Start and other childhood programs were embraced as the solution. Early childhood programs demonstrated many children suffered from an assortment of undiagnosed medical and dental conditions. These conditions, in some instances, affected the child's ability to function in school. Screening children for tuberculosis, malnutrition, tooth decay, and variety of neurological disorders would be put into operation before the end of the decade.

The designation "learning disabilities" was wholeheartedly accepted by middle-class parents who did not like the designation "emotional problems" attached to their children. To the child or parent, there was no stigma attached to the learning disabilities label. The child, beginning in the 1970s, was disabled and was incapable of meeting the demands of school curriculum. The child and his disability, not the system, would now be the focus of remediation.

The 1970's witnessed a surge by psychologists and psychiatrists in studying and diagnosing attention problems in children. By the end of the decade there were over two thousand published studies on attention deficits. In 1980, the American Psychiatric Association endorsed "attention deficit disorder" by listing it in the influential *Diagnostic and Statistical Manual of Mental Disorders III* (DSM III). The manual was revised in 1987 (DSM III-R) with the now familiar acronym ADHD. The parent advocacy group Children and Adults with Attention Deficit Disorder (CH.A.D.D) swelled from twenty-nine chapters in 1988 to over six hundred in 1994. By the mid-nineties, with the publication of Edward M. Hallowell's and John J. Ratey's best selling book *Driven to Distraction* and a July 18, 1994 article in *Time* magazine, attention deficit hyperactive disorder became an undisputed neurological disease in the minds of many Americans.

Behavior: A Public Health Problem

On December 30, 1969 a letter from Arnold A. Hutschnecker, a New York physician, was delivered to the Secretary of Health, Education and Welfare via the President's domestic affairs advisor, John Ehrlichman. President Nixon was soliciting his opinion on the "mass testing" of all 6 – 8 year old children in order to identify those who have violent, or other anti-social predispositions. "Treatment" would be provided for children identified with delinquent tendencies. Attacking the problem of violent crime, according to Hutschnecker, was to focus on "the criminal mind of the child" and "to prevent a child with a delinquent character structure from being allowed to grow into a full-fledged teenage delinquent or adult criminal."[42]

A reply was drafted in February 1970 by the director of the National Institute of Mental Health, Dr. Stanley F. Yolles. Dr. Yolles stated a number of problems associated with such an approach to crime prevention; the most significant being no reliable way to predict future behavior. In addition, to intervene in the lives of children and their families based on *predicted* behavior would have obvious social policy and constitutional implications.

---

[42] Peter Schrag and Diane Divoky, *The Myth of the Hyperactive Child*, (New York, NY: Dell Publishing Co., 1975), p.17, 18.

On April 14, 1970, James Allen, Jr., then assistant Secretary for Education, and U.S. Commissioner of Education spoke at the National School Board Association proposing a program of education, health and welfare of every child. Under his plan school districts would have a "Central Diagnostic Center" where parents would bring their preschool children for an educational and medical evaluation and diagnosis. The goal was to create for every child an individualized program of education. Allen's proposal was far more sweeping and intrusive into the lives of children and their families than was Hutschnecker's. Greater faith was put on testing and treatment for the purpose of curing and preventing delinquency. No one could condemn his motive.

The Hutschnecker and Allen proposals did not have an immediate impact on social or education policy; however, the ground was prepared for a profound change in ideology and practice. Within three years, the San Francisco Unified School District would pull Allen's proposal off the shelf and use it to create a program to test and "treat" all children starting at age three. Hutschnecker's concepts would be embedded in programs to identify "pre-delinquents" in Southern California. Similar statewide projects to test for medical and psychological problems would be created in Illinois and Maryland. By the mid-1970s Hutschnecker's and Allen's proposals would have influenced millions of children through research programs, teacher training courses, experiments in behavior modification, and conferences on delinquency and learning disabilities.

The focus shifted from reforming the institution (schools) in the late 1950's and 1960's to reforming the individual in the late 1970's. Delinquent teens that grew up to be lawless adults, opposed to society and its institutions, were the problem. Medical metaphors that emphasized "prescriptions, diagnosis, 'treatment' of patients," replaced sociological language which had already replaced biblical language. Sinful or mal-behavior, like a disease, was the purview of modern medical science. A nation-wide program of crime prevention, led by "trained professionals" who offer "effective remedies," was underway. Testing scales were designed that enabled the "professional" to determine learning disabilities, delinquent tendencies or a multitude of other problems. The tests were not only used to justify placement in existing programs or school grades, but to create new categories and labels which had no basis other than the test itself. The essence of an individual's psyche, abilities and personality could be understood in purely "scientific" terms. Normal childhood behavior as observed by parents ("the kid won't sit still") turned into hyperkinesis, minimal brain dysfunction, and later ADHD. Instead of creating tests to discover diseases, diseases were created for the outcomes of the tests. Symptoms became syndromes and syndromes became diseases. Within a period of five years beginning in 1969 an epidemic of "learning disorders," juvenile delinquencies and other juvenile pathology swept the nation. Treatments which included punishment, psychoactive drugs or counseling and behavior modification were being sought for those "illnesses," Whereas it was once the system that needed changing, now it was the individual who was having trouble living within the system who needs to change. Responsibility to help the individual to change would fall on the system or State; therefore, the State would take the role as physician. Schools would serve as "clinics" providing psychosocial "treatment" for individuals. In a January, 1969 article in *Today's Education*, the official magazine for the National Education Association, entitled "Forecast for the 70's," the authors said "it should be more accurate to term (the teacher) a 'learning clinician.' Schools were thought of as being clinics where psychosocial treatments were dispensed to the individual.

A steady stream of research, tending to be more scientism than science, poured from universities and child study centers. Deficient statistical methods, tilted population samples, small control groups, and the absence of long-range follow up flawed the studies. To make matters worse, the research was all built on a foundation of totally arbitrary definitions which, in most cases, represented nothing more than the bias of mental health and school officials translated into scientific jargon. However, in some cases, there were genuine forms of pathology requiring special attention by teachers, parents and physicians. These included hearing and speech problems and mental retardation, which all possess organic abnormalities as their cause. It was these demonstrable disorders along with shrinking norms of acceptable childhood behavior that conveniently provided a believable rationale for the inventing of other "diseases" defined by society and not by empirical evidence. Real diseases became models for creating new ones. If corporal punishment or expelling a child from school was no longer an option, at least parents could be encouraged or forced to find a physician who would prescribe the appropriate medication to control the child's unacceptable behavior. All this was done in the name of prevention and social good. A hyperactive child was seen as a pre-delinquent, thus he must be treated for the good of society-at-large.

The logical outcome was to bring as many individuals into the program and at the earliest age possible. It is consistent with the old adage, "an ounce of prevention is worth a pound of cure", the earlier the diagnosis, the better for everyone. The child can be treated appropriately and the teacher will not have the nuisance or menace to deal with in the classroom. The idea is to identify problem children before they are loosed onto the streets to commit havoc. Of course, the word *control* is carefully avoided. It is a word that smacks of "big brother," politics and manipulation. Nevertheless, the goal of the ideology was a sterile state cleansed of those who won't behave, are difficult, peculiar, or nonconformists, because they infect the culture and its institutions.

The traditional way of controlling children included the humiliation of a paddling, detention or expulsion. The system in those days was personal and overt. There was no question as to who was doing what to whom. It was not based on the assumption of what the child might do in the future, but on what the child did today. Most significantly, the child was not a victim of wacky neurons or chemicals, but was recognized as having a choice; therefore, he was responsible for his behavior.

The new mode of control, which was primarily directed at children, insists it is more effective and humane. Is not identifying and treating problems before they ripen into full blown delinquency inarguably better? Who would deny behavior modification and/or medication is better than punishment and failure? After all, we would do great harm to the child by damaging his delicate self-esteem. The new mode assumes the problem is worse than the remedy; however, it always leaves the definition of "worse" to the person in charge of the therapy or "cure." The accuser (school official, psychologists, etc.) is empowered and has the prerogative of defining and determining future behavior on the basis of present "diagnosis." Masquerading as science, noncompliance is touted to be a disease or malfunctioning of the brain and the individual is stripped of his rights to challenge or assert himself. The line is blurred between poor academic performance, crime and disease.

The legitimacy of the system, with its diagnosis and therapies, does not depend on results any more than did the witch doctor dancing around the fire and mumbling incoherently. The power came from the routine itself (testing, diagnosing, creation of programs and treatments) - the mystification. What the buffalo horns, face paint and bonfire did for the witch doctor, the *Diagnostic and Statistical Manual of Mental Disorders,* syndromes, illnesses and interventions can do for the diagnostician. The point, after all, is the confirmation of it own legitimacy.

Federal Violence Initiative

To contend with growing violence the *Federal Violence Initiative* was proposed in the early 1970s. Government agencies were funding psychiatrists who claimed that urban uprisings were caused by genetic defects and brain disease. Government funds were used to establish urban medical institutes devoted to violence research and treatment. However, it was not until 1992 that the government's highest ranking psychiatrist, Fredrick Goodwin, proposed a "violence prevention initiative" for the purpose of identifying children with presumed biological and genetic defects making them predisposed to violent behavior. If their "illness" could be diagnosed and treated, society may be spared a large percentage of violent crime and the costs incurred by these crimes. Such a program, according to Goodwin, would require the use of public schools for screening purposes. A nine-page document, proposing a "new initiative" and "plan" for violence prevention was prepared for the 1994 budget.

Goodwin's programs, as well as other similar proposals for massive psychiatric interventions, were highly criticized. While the immediate threat was no longer present, the idea regarding genetic vulnerability and biochemical imbalances as the cause of social problems remained. Federally funded research and lobbying by the biomedical research community and the pharmaceutical industry continued unabated. Children's disorders and disruptive or violent behavior in particular were huge markets. Giant pharmaceutical companies and the mental health profession stood to profit enormously.

On April 20, 1999, eighteen year old Eric Harris and seventeen year old Dylan Klebold led an assault on their own high school in Littleton, Colorado. They killed or wounded thirty-five people. On April 28, 1999, a high school boy opened fire killing one student and seriously wounding another at W.R. Myers High School in Alberta, Canada. Four teenagers were arrested on May 4, 1999, before they carried out plans to attack Adams City High School near Denver, Colorado. Again in May of 1999, four boys in the suburban Port Huron, Michigan area were arrested for planning an assault that would outdo the Columbine catastrophe. On May 20, 1999, fifteen year old T.J. Solomon entered Heritage High School in Conyers, Georgia and shot and wounded six classmates. On June 7, 1999, a solution was proposed when President Clinton and Vice-President Gore and their wives came together with leading figures in the field of biological psychiatry. These "experts" spoke of how children suffering from genetic and biological brain diseases may become mentally stressed and potentially violent. The President concluded the conference by announcing a multi-federal initiative that would help identify troubled children and get them into a treatment program. The use of the nation's schools, according to the President and other speakers, would be of paramount importance in identifying children and referring them for psychiatric evaluation. Not one speaker mentioned that Harris and Solomon were at the time of the shootings under psychiatric care and on medication (Harris was taking a Prozac[R]-like drug called Luvox[R]. Solomon was taking Ritalin[R]).

On April 29, 2002, President George W. Bush established the New Freedom Commission on Mental Health (NFC). The commission's mission was to review mental health care in the United States. The following year, the NFC released its findings and recommendations to screen every American for mental illness. The report focused on children's mental health and the need for mental health check-ups and school-based mental health care. TeenScreen,[TM] a controversial mental health screening program developed by Columbia University's Child Psychiatry Research Department, was recommended as a "model program." This program, and many others like it, would be a windfall for psychiatrists, pharmaceutical companies and schools who want to control children without providing real help for their problems. Children's supposed flawed brains would take adults off the proverbial hook and using fake scientific solutions, hang children on the same hook.

The reduction of human behavior to an expression of DNA or a wholly biological event is dangerous and unbiblical. Medical and psychiatric explanations, cloaked in pseudo-science and the language of disease and healing, is difficult for the man on the street to discern. Promises of success may be uncritically embraced by a public enthusiastic to find seemingly humane medical solutions for violence. Nowhere in the discussion does one find words like sin. Moreover, school shootings and violence remain a regular news item despite the millions of dollars and multitude of commissions and programs. The psychiatrists are a failure and the lives of children are at even greater risk.

No Proof of Disease

Once psychiatry entered the schools via federal legislation, educational psychiatry became a huge industry. As funds for special education increased, so did the number of children found to have "learning disabilities." The term "learning disabled" simply means that despite normal or above intelligence, the student, for some reason cannot read. Researchers at the University of Michigan reported that eighty-five percent of the students previously identified as normal would have been classified as learning disabled under one of the assessment tools used. Teachers have been so indoctrinated with the idea that slow learners have something inherently wrong with them, that in a 1981 nationwide survey they considered 57.7 percent of all students defective and in need of special extracurricular help.[43]

Regna Lee Wood, a woman who began her teaching career shortly after World War II, commenting on the high percentage of students labeled LD said, "These grim statistics show that 80 percent of the Special Education students were born seventy years too late. For virtually all of the 4 million with normal intelligence and no limiting physical disabilities could and would have learned to read in regular first- and second-grade phonics classes in the twenties and early thirties. Proof is in the scores of 17 million academic military tests taken by World War II registrants who could read at today's fifth-grade level.[44]

The mental health community does not have as simple a view of the problem. They look at these children as being sick. Psychiatrist Robert Castel wrote, "It is common knowledge that the American educational system is particularly inefficient in some areas. Perhaps this is why cause and effect are often reversed, and pupils are made responsible for the poor performance of the school system—a conspicuous example of blaming the victim. More than in other countries, there is in the United States a tendency to diagnose failure and maladjustment as effects of individual problems or maladies, and psychological therapy and/or

---

[43] *Right to Read Report*, April/May 1994, p.4.
[44] *Right to Read Report*, January 1994, p. 3.

drugs are then prescribed as appropriate treatments."[45] The nail in the coffin was when psychiatry listed a variety of learning difficulties as mental disorders in the DSM. The disorders are *Arithmetic Learning Disorder, Developmental Expressive Disorder, Writing Disorder,* and *Developmental Reading Disorder.*

The most pervasive diagnostic labeling of children is Attention Deficit Disorder. It is currently listed in the DSM-IV-TR as ADHD or Attention Deficit Hyperactive Disorder. Neurologist, Fred A. Baughman in a letter to the editor of *Pediatrics* magazine wrote: "The AAP's clinical practice guideline[46] opens: "Attention-deficit/hyperactive disorder (ADHD) is the most common neurobehavioral disorder of childhood." "Neurobehavioral" implies an abnormality of the brain; a disease. And yet, no confirmatory, diagnostic abnormality has been found. With six million children said to have it, most of them on addictive, dangerous stimulants, ambiguity as to the scientific status of ADHD is not acceptable. Goodwin[47] acknowledged the 'narrow definition of disease that requires the presence of a biological abnormality.' Carey[48] testified at the 1998 Consensus Conference (CC): 'What is now most often described as ADHD in the United States appears to be a set of normal behavioral variations... This discrepancy leaves the validity of the construct in doubt...' The CC Panel[49] concluded: 'We do not have an independent, valid test for ADHD, and there are no data to indicate that ADHD is due to a brain malfunction.' More recently, Castellanos[50] confessed: 'Incontrovertible evidence is still lacking!' Where has the notion come from that it is a disease? Carey observed: 'ADHD behaviors are assumed to be largely or entirely due to abnormal brain function. The DSM-IV does not say so, but textbooks and journals do.' Later in the conference, Carey

---

[45] Robert Castel, Francoise Castel and Anne Lovell, *The Psychiatric Society*, (New York, NY: Columbia University Press, 1982), p. 205.

[46] American Academy of Pediatrics, Committee on Quality Improvement and Subcommittee on Attention Deficit/Hyperactive Disorder Clinical Practice: diagnosis and evaluation of the child with attention deficit/hyperactive disorder. *Pediatrics.* 2000; 105:1158-1170.

[47] D. Goodwin, *Is Alcoholism Hereditary?* (New York, NY: Ballatine Books, 1989).

[48] W.B. Carey, Is attention deficit hyperactive disorder a valid disorder? Invited presentation to the NIH Consensus Development Conference on ADHD; November 16-18, 1998; National Institutes of Mnetal Health; Bethesda, MD.

[49] NIH Consensus Development Conference on ADHD (transcript). November 16-18, 1998; National Institutes of Health; Bethesda, MD.

[50] J. Pekkanen, *Making Sense of Ritalin*, (interview of F.X. Castellanos). Readers Digest, January, 2000 p. 159-168.

issued the plea: 'We see... that the causes of these behaviors called ADHD are entirely speculative. And yet... parents and children are being told that these behaviors are due to a brain malfunction. Can you not please strengthen the statement to discourage practitioners from making this statement when there is not adequate proof to support that at this time?' ... It is apparent that virtually all professionals of the extended ADHD 'industry' convey to parents, and to the public-at-large, that ADHD is a 'disease' and that children said to have it are 'diseased' and 'abnormal.' This is a perversion of the scientific record and a violation of the informed consent rights of all patients and of the public-at-large. The wording of the AAP guideline should be changed..."[51]

The only physical complications of an ADHD diagnosis are related to stimulant medication. Unlike all other risks versus benefit analyses in medicine, there is never an actual disease on the risk side. The American Psychiatric Association responded to similar criticisms of various mental "diseases" on September 26, 2003. The APA released an arrogant statement on the diagnosis and treatment of mental disorders saying, "...the lack of a diagnostic laboratory test capable of confirming the presence of a mental disorder constituted evidence that these disorders are not medically valid. ...the American Psychiatric Association (APA) respects the right of individuals to express their impatience with the pace of science..."

The argument is not whether the APA has a test or does not have a test to diagnose ADHD. The issue that leads to the conclusion that no disease exists is there lacks an abnormality for which to test. It is not that their critics are "impatient with the pace of science." The issue is producing the proof of disease. If the APA gives even an inch on the disease debate, the resultant cracks in its foundation may well, bring down the entire profession. As such, no quarter will be given.

Psychiatry and Psychology: Specialists in Education?

"Experimental psychology," founded in 1879 by materialist German psychologist Wilhelm Wundt declared man to be an animal with no soul, whose thoughts, emotions and feelings were nothing more than brain chemistry. The traditional view of man where man was held accountable for his behavior, changed drastically as a result.

---

[51] Fred A. Baughman, *Diagnosis and Evaluation of the Child With Attention Deficit/Hyperactive Disorder*, (*Pediatrics*, Vol. 107 No. 5, May 2001), p. 139.

The concept of "free will," was considered to be religious superstition. This colossal shift of man's view of himself would have enormous consequences. According to Wundt, man's conduct was a result of causes beyond his individual control.

Wundt's theories found their way into education through men like Edward Lee Thorndike. Thorndike studied the mechanisms of learning by observing rats, chickens and cats. He extrapolated his finding to human beings made in the image and likeness of God. There was no question concerning Thorndike's intentions when he wrote: "It will, of course, be understood that directly or indirectly, soon or late, every advance in the sciences of human nature will contribute to our success in controlling human nature..."[52] A reading program developed by James Cattell called "Whole Word" or "Look-say" was an example of one of Thorndike's "advances." The program ignored phonics and required children to memorize words without understanding the sequence of letters or sounds. The method was meant to make reading easier, but actually served to confuse children. The result was a disaster. Many children developed reading problems or didn't learn to read at all. Critics of the plan accurately predicted SAT scores would plummet and functional illiteracy would soar. Unfortunately, the educational establishment clung to the new method for some time. They ignored the tried-and-true phonics method of teaching because it didn't fit in with the prevailing psychological ideologies in education. Our society is still suffering today as a result.

Clifford W. Beers has often been referred to as the founder of the modern mental health movement. Beers created the National Committee on Mental Hygiene in 1909. This was the beginning of psychiatry's claim of authority on human behavior and the right to interfere with school and family for the public good. It was the Mental Hygiene movement that first popularized the psychiatric idea that poverty causes crime and criminals are not responsible for what they do. The committee formed the "Program for the Prevention of Delinquency" and played a significant role in developing "child guidance clinics" around the world. His program to prevent delinquency propelled Mental Hygiene concepts into public education. Ralph Truitt, the head of the Committee's Division of Child Guidance Clinics in 1927, wrote: "If we are going to prevent dependency, delinquency, insanity, and

---

[52] Merle L. Borrowman, *Teacher Education in America*, (Richmon, VA: William Byrd Press, Inc., 1965), p. 177. (Education Booklet text, cite 11 in the book).

general inadequacy, the school should be the focus of our attack."[53] Psychiatrist John R. Rees, co-founder of the World Federation for Mental Health, left no doubt of the objective of him and his peers when he said: "We have made a useful attack upon a number of professions. The two easiest of them naturally are the teaching profession and the church; the two most difficult are law and medicine."[54]

Psychological programs known jointly as Outcome Based Education were introduced in the public schools in the 1960s and 1970s. Psychologists claimed there were three sources of stress in children's experience related to school: school failure itself, curriculum centered on academics, and disciplinary procedures. These problems were said to be the leading cause of low self-esteem, truancy and bad behavior. Educator Alan Larson, former Secretary of the Oregon Federation of Independent Schools said, "This whole emphasis on stress in schools is based on the psychiatric principle that standards are bad, and they are bad because they produce stress. The only way you can run up any stress is if you run into a standard that you are having trouble measuring up to. That is the producer of stress. Therefore, the whole stress thing was just another little channel in this whole overall campaign to get at standards."[55]

In the forties and fifties psychologist Carl Rogers pioneered what he a called client-centered method of therapy. Rogers counseling approach was based on the assumption that a person's "real self," which is basically good, tends to be repressed, but can be released under certain conditions. The condition, "unconditional positive regard" is when the therapist completely accepts the client's values and behavior in a non-judgmental way. Rogers method struck a chord within and outside of therapeutic circles. Much of our current talk about "not imposing values" on other people is borrowed from Rogers' therapeutic vocabulary. The therapist's main role is to allow the client to find his own direction and answers within himself. The assumption is if the therapist can point the client in the right direction, his natural healthy instincts will lead him in the right way. Client-centered therapy is also referred to as "non-directive counseling."

---

[53] B.K. Eakman, *Cloning of the American Mind, Eradicating Morality Through Education*, (Lafayette, LA: Huntington House Publishers, 1998), p. 380.
[54] John Rawlings Rees, *Strategic Planning for Mental Health*, Mental Health Vol. 1, No. 4, Oct. 1940, p. 104.
[55] Bruce Wiseman, *Psychiatry The Ultimate Betrayal*, (Los Angeles, CA: Freedom Publishing, 1995), pp. 281-282.

Rogers and others began to think how non-directive counseling principles could be used in classrooms to teach children. Rogers wrote about non-directive teaching. Non-directive teaching was not teaching in the traditional sense at all. The teacher's job was to facilitate self-expression and enhance self-esteem.

Moral education, which was taught years ago, was replaced by another more "scientific" approach. The new approach was called "decision making" or "moral reasoning" or "Values Clarification." The developers of Values Clarification, an outgrowth of the human potential movement in psychology, had merely taken Carl Rogers' non-directive, non-judgmental approach and applied them to moral education. Teachers did not teach values, but provided an atmosphere (non-judgmental, etc) where the student felt comfortable to clarify his own values. Values Clarifications, true to it's human potential movement origins, puts a heavy emphasis on feelings. The Values Clarification handbook *Twenty Things You Love to Do* emphasizes the prominence of feelings and virtually equates them to values. A value is essentially what you like to do, not what you ought to do.

The marriage between psychology and education led to a plethora of "educational psychology" courses that soon overran the curriculum of teacher training. Content level curriculum was siphoned away by non-subject education courses on how to teach children to adjust, express their true feelings and esteem themselves. The teacher was not someone who would ensure that children would learn the three R's, but a pseudo-social worker and pseudo-counselor. Teaching was no longer simply disseminating information for children to remember while learning to read and write. The stress was on critical thinking instead of memorizing facts. The emphasis was no longer on the content of the Gettysburg Address or the Bill of Rights, but on a child's feelings, attitudes, emotions and beliefs toward those documents or their authors.[56]

Most teachers are dedicated individuals who love children. However, many are unaware that these "innovative" curriculums are nothing more than old ideas with a long and sad history, having undergone a name change and a periodic cosmetic facelift. With

---

[56] This has crept into the church as well as we have moved away from "what the Bible says" to "what the Bible says...to me" This postmodern move is from objective truth to subjective or relative conjecture. "Thy Word is Truth", plain and simple. God does not need anyone else's subjective feelings in order to communicate His truth to every generation.

little sense of history, they are in a poor position to evaluate new developments in education or to distinguish the "in-thing" from genuine educational advances. Unfortunately, the result is predictable; education keeps recycling its errors. Failed ideas and theories keep popping up under new names and no one notices.

"Education specialists" over the years have all been behavioral psychologists or psychiatrists. They were men (or women) trying to bring what was then the cutting edge of science to the study of how humans learn. In their endeavor to uncover scientific truth, they attempted to discard the "religious superstitions" of their forefathers. From Wilhelm Wundt, who is credited with making psychology a "true science;" Edward Lee Thorndike, who concluded animals learn by trial and error, reward or punishment and human beings, being highly evolved animals, learn the same way; John Dewey's "progressive education" ideas, Carl Rogers nondirective teaching, to today's most advanced mental health care professionals, psychology and psychiatry are the rudders guiding the system. Arm in arm with their predecessors, under the auspices of science, they have become ensconced in positions of authority in American education.

The Consequences of Calling Behavior a Disease

The psychological point of view, teaching that human beings are just physical and chemical machines, cannot simply be dismissed by Christians as strange and amusing. It is too important, too pervasive, and ultimately the consequences are too far-reaching. In Jeremy Leven's novel *Satan, His Psychotherapy and Cure by the Unfortunate Doctor Kassler*, the Devil complains, "Psychotherapy worries the hell out of me... It keeps turning evil into neurosis and explaining away people's behavior with drives and complexes... Modern psychiatry is putting me out of business."[57]

Psychology's grip on our culture has gone a long way toward explaining the undeniable erosion of personal values so evident in America today. Every aspect of society has been infected, even the church. In order for psychology to accomplish it's self-actualizing goal with it's emphasis on autonomy, feelings, emotions, and self-esteem, it moved sin and deviant behavior out of the category of sin

---

[57] Jeremy Leven, *Satan, His Psychotherapy and Cure by the Unfortunate Doctor Kassler*, (New York, NY: 1982), p. 466.

and placed it in the category of sickness. For example, the sexual sinner that Paul wrote about (1 Corinthians 2:13) became the sex addict. The thief (1 Corinthians 2:14) became the kleptomaniac. The drunkard (1 Corinthians 6: 10) became the alcoholic. The rebellious child (2 Timothy 3:2) became afflicted with Attention Deficit Disorder" or "Oppositional Defiant Disorder." A family in which the husband will not work, the wife will not keep the home and the children will not obey are no longer considered a sinful family. They have become a dysfunctional family. The liar became a compulsive liar. The gambler became a compulsive gambler. The idolater became a person who suffers from an obsessive-compulsive disorder. The "deeds of the flesh... which are immorality impurity, sensuality, idolatry, sorcery, enmities, strife, jealousy, outbursts of anger, disputes, dissensions, factions, envying, drunkenness, carousing" (Galatians 5:19-21) have all been redefined using psychopathological words.[58]

The insidious spread of psychology, calling sin sickness, into the church is the reason evangelicalism counts for so little in the modern world. The church is confused concerning the nature of man and his behavior. One cannot understand the problems we face today unless one realizes the thinking of the vast majority of Christians is governed and determined by what they regard as science. Psychology, it is believed, has the diagnosis for all our problems. Man is explained in terms of the resultant operation and interaction of various forces, biological, chemical, and others. We contend this has led to the present conduct and behavior of men and women, Christian men and women, included. This has led to what is commonly referred to as "diminished responsibility". In other words, if a man has the "disease" of alcoholism then he is not responsible for his drunkenness. If a child has Attention Deficit Disorder he is not responsible for his selfishness and disruptive behavior in the classroom. The inevitable result is a drastic decline of morality and godliness.[59]

Psychiatry's materialistic, anti-Judeo-Christian slant; while it would strike against the very root of our culture, would nevertheless survive and prosper. In 1945, G. Brock Chisholm, past president of the World Federation for Mental Health, said, "The re-interpretation and eventually *eradication* of the concept of right and wrong which has been the basis of child training, the *substitution* of intelligent and

---

[58] For a more thorough study on this subject read *Deceptive Diagnosis: When Sin Is Called Sickness*, by David Tyler and Kurt Grady (Focus Publishing, Bemidji, MN. 1-800-913-6287 or www.focuspublishing.com).

[59] *Ibid*., p. 121.

rational thinking for faith in the certainties of the old people, these are the belated objectives of practically all effective psychotherapy." He added, "The fact is, that most psychiatrists and psychologists and other respectable people have escaped from these moral chains and are able to observe and think freely."[60] Even more significant are his words, "We have swallowed all manner of poisonous certainties fed us by our parents, our Sunday and day school teachers, our politicians, our priests, our newspapers and others with a vested interest in controlling us. 'Thou shalt become as gods, knowing good and evil,' good and evil with which to keep children under control, with which to prevent free thinking, with which to impose local and familial and national loyalties and with which to blind children to their glorious intellectual heritage." Chisholm laid out an agenda for his peers when he said, "If the race is to be freed from its crippling burden of good and evil, it must be psychiatrists who take the original responsibility."[61]

An example of the eradication of right and wrong is seen in the introduction of Values Clarification in 1984 by the U.S. Department of Education. The program included a handbook of seventy-nine strategies for teachers and students. Included in the book was a seven-step procedure which allowed the child to first "thaw out" previous values instilled in him through family and church relationships. The student was instructed to set these values aside, consider and select a new set of values which he felt was important to him. The third step was to make these newly-chosen values part of his lifestyle. Some of the questions included:

> How many of you think there are times when cheating is justified?
>
> How many of you approve of premarital sex for boys?
>
> How many of you approve of premarital sex for girls?
>
> How many of you would approve of a marriage between homosexuals being sanctioned by a priest, minister or rabbi?
>
> How many of you would approve of a young couple trying out a marriage by living together for six months before actually getting married?

---

[60] G. Brock Chisholm, *The Reestablishmnet of Peacetime Society---The William Alanson White Memorial Lectures, Second Series, Psychiatry: Journal of the Biology and the Pathology of Interpersonal Relations*, February 1946, p. 9.
[61] *Ibid.*, pp. 7,9.

The relativism sweeping across America was turned loose in the classroom through Values Clarifications. No standard was offered to equate one's values to and no suggestion that some values might be better than others was given. Values Clarifications mixed up trivial questions ("Do you like to read?") with important ethical issues ("Do you approve of premarital sex?"). While the term values clarifications is not used so much today, it is nevertheless still with us in curriculums and the relativistic language we hear so often.

Psychologist Lawrence Kohlberg gave Values Clarifications competition with his moral reasoning approach. Kohlberg rejected character education. He wanted to teach children to be moral thinkers by teaching them a *process* of moral reasoning. It was still up to the children to make their own decisions about morality; however, their decisions would be based on reason. In this model the teacher poses a dilemma and encourages an exchange of ideas and opinions. Instead of spending classroom time talking about the virtues of honesty, loyalty, and self-control and how to practice them in everyday life dilemmas were presented where honesty may not be the best policy or where honesty and loyalty might conflict or where stealing or killing may be a legitimate course of action.

The developers of these and other psychologized curriculums, past and present, proceed on the basis of a dubious assumption. They seemingly assume that such things as honesty, loyalty and self-control are highly valued by children and do not have to be taught. The only difficulty they seem to see is choosing between values that conflict with one another. They assume children have a natural goodness which will always lead them in the direction of deciding to do the right thing. The only problem is getting in touch with one's feelings or of learning to reason things out. Helping children get in touch with their feelings and training them to reason things out is the job of the teacher – facilitator.

Psychiatry and psychology have become something of a substitute for "old-fashioned, archaic" belief systems of right or wrong, good or bad. People, who years ago, took comfort from the words of God now take comfort from the words of Freud, Wundt, Rogers and a host of others. In the past, the common reference point was the Bible. Today, it is the therapeutic language and theories of modern-day people-changers. Instead of providing solutions their "remedies" have exasperated society's problems. For example, sex education has not been able to curtail sexual activity among teenagers in America. Why? It was never intended to do so. Non-judgmental sex education, where everybody's view is legitimate, does not condemn, in a way a teenager would take seriously, early sexuality. Sex education is based on the expectation that teenagers will be sexually active. Even though abstinence was grafted into the nondirective method, it was only one of many choices. The object is to provide an atmosphere where the young person can make a decision based on what is right for him or her. What is right is what he chooses for himself. Choice, not choosing the right thing, but having the right to choose is the premier value.

The current moral education classroom has a lot in common with the television talk show. These programs thrive on the exchange of ideas and opinions. The ground rules are clear, all views are legitimate. All points of view and behaviors must be tolerated. Tolerance and open-mindedness is the chief virtue. The dilemma of the television talk show and the classroom is nobody has objective criteria for deciding right and wrong. The criterion is what "feels right to me." Time and energy is spent on exchanging ideas and exploring feelings, but there is no moral guidance or forming of character. The virtues are not explained or discussed. No models of good behavior or heroes are provided. No reason is given why a person should want to be good. Students are given nothing to live by or look up to. They learn that even the most basic values are matters of dispute. They infer morality is something you talk about in class, but is not something you live.

The old Judeo-Christian morality conflicts with psychiatry's agenda as is evidence by Chisholm's words and others. In 1960, Mrs. Joseph Bean, the wife of a Glendale, California, school district trustee in a scathing address before her husband's board of education spoke to the issue of morals. "The traditional philosophy of education," she said, "recognizes that there are absolute truths, eternal truths, immutable truths, and that the school is vitally interested in transmitting these absolutes to our young." She continued, "Without official recognition and without official adoption a new philosophy has largely replaced the official one in this country's schools. This philosophy is behaviorism and holds that man is not responsible for his actions, that he is a victim of his environment and not accountable for his acts."[62]

---

[62] Bruce Wiseman, *Psychiatry The Ultimate Betrayal*, (Los Angeles, CA: Freedom Publishing, 1995), p. 16.

In light of the beliefs and practices of psychiatry and psychology, it should be no surprise that there is a moral crisis in our children, schools, and society as a whole. G. Brock Chisholm's dream of the "eventual eradication of the concept of right and wrong" has made remarkable advances in our day. In an address to the Childhood International Education Seminar, psychiatrist Chester M. Pierce claimed in 1973, "Every child in America entering school at the age of five is insane because he comes to school with certain allegiances to our founding fathers, toward our elected officials, toward his parents, toward a belief in a supernatural being, and toward the sovereignty of this nation as a separate entity. It's up to you as teachers to make all these sick children well by creating the international child of the future."

Psychology did not formally emerge until the mid-to late 19th century, first in Europe, and then in America. Certain nineteenth–century influences made a strong impression on the emerging field. One of the foremost influences was the work of Charles Darwin (1809-1882) whose elucidation of a theory of natural selection in evolution revolutionized scientific thought. His 1859 seminal work, *On the Origin of Species*, broadly influenced Western intellectual circles, and his later works on the descent of humans and the expression of emotions in humans and animals became cornerstone literature in the fledging field of psychology."[63] To the extent that Darwinism and psychology as a whole, with its relativism, emphasis on feelings, emotions, and self-esteem, made advances into our culture and schools, morals declined. What appeared to be benign secularism has left us without absolutes or at least some kind of official standards. Relativism has become a fundamental assumption. Ironically, almost all teachers, when it comes to concrete moral situations, take a non-relativistic approach. When a child's notebook has been stolen, teachers don't lapse into rhetoric about "not imposing values." They insist the person responsible confess and return the stolen notebook.

The influence of psychology in the classroom has mushroomed over the past several decades with no sign of abating. Thomas K. Fagan, Professor and Coordinator of School Psychology Programs at Memphis State University, studies the growth in number of school psychologists and estimated their growth as follows in 1993:

---

[63] *Ibid.*, pp. 24, 25.

Psychologists in Schools

1920 200

1940 500

1950 1000

1960 3000

1970 5000

1980 10,000

1990 ..... 22,000[64]

A recent study indicates, "A shortage of school psychologists has existed for a number of years... Such a shortage also existed in the late 1980s; it seemed to briefly remit but began increasing again in the mid-1990s. It has shown no signs of remission since that time. ...the shortage of school psychologists will increase over the next several years and peak in about 2010."[65] All indicators agree the employment outlook for school psychologists is very favorable.

Psychology, bringing its muddy relativism to classroom discussions, will continue to be a major player in education and the lack of morality in America. "There is no question regarding the arrival and maturation of the field, which has evolved into a large and potent force. Although school psychology is still small in comparison with its larger parent fields, there is no denying that it has made significant inroads in influence and that school psychologists are shaping practice, policy, and science at all levels—from the local school to the highest decision-making bodies."[66]

The Frog in the Kettle

On the first day of an elementary psychology course at Johns Hopkins University [in the 1950s]; a professor sat on his desk silently reading the morning newspaper. The bell rang, but he didn't seem to notice it. Then audibly he began to read the headlines of the front page articles. They captioned difficult world problems,

---

[64] Bruce Wiseman, *Psychiatry The Ultimate Betrayal*, (Los Angeles, CA: Freedom Publishing, 1995), p. 287.

[65] Kenneth W. Merrell, Ruth A. Ervin, Gretchen A. Gimmpel, *School Psychology for the 21st Century*, (New York, NY: The Guilford Press, 2006), p. 109.

[66] *Ibid*, p. 266.

spoke of inhuman acts of man to his fellow man, and, in general, painted the typical sensational front page picture one may read every day. Presently, he looked up and said, "The world is in a mess." He spent the rest of the hour explaining how psychology is the world's one hope for straightening out that mess.[67]

In spite of the fact that bit by bit psychology and psychiatry has succeeded in entering our homes, courts, legislature, workplaces, and schools, the newspaper headlines have not changed. Lawlessness, greed, school violence, decay of moralities, abuse of all kinds, drunkenness, drugs, disintegration of the family, divorce, teenage pregnancies have all increased significantly. In fact, things are worse than anyone could have imagined back in the 1950s.

Our cultural norms, which characterized our society for generations, have undergone a drastic change. The basic concepts of right or wrong, according to psychiatry's best minds, can no longer be considered the foundation of an ordered society. Instead, they are supposedly the causes of individual stress, guilt, anxiety and depression. Children are being taught they are their own authority on questions of morals and values. The Judeo-Christian ethic, once a pervasive and guiding moral influence, has been subjected to the same wind of change. The Bible is widely criticized as being harmful, unscientific and therefore ill-equipped to address the problems people experience in the real world. The culture is openly hostile toward believers, scoffing at traditions and beliefs. Virtue is held up to ridicule. An honest man is viewed as a foolish man. Criminal behavior is excused; the public is expected to be sympathetic to the supposed "insanities" suffered by murderers, child abusers, and other criminals. Sinful and deviant behavior is called sickness. The drunkard is an alcoholic, the thief is a kleptomaniac, the rebellious child has oppositional defiant disorder, or ADHD. What ideology, in the name of intellectual enlightenment, has seeped into our thinking?

"Psychiatry is probably the single most destructive force that has effected the American society within the last fifty years"[68]

---

[67] Jay E. Adams, *Competent to Counsel* (Philipsburg, NJ: Presbyterian and Reformed Publishing Complany, 1970), p. 1.

[68] Bruce Wiseman, *Psychiatry: The Ultimate Betrayal* (Los Angeles, CA: Freedom Publishing, 1995), p. 6.

This statement does not come from a uniformed individual. These are the words of a 1993 interview with of Dr. Thomas Szasz, Professor of Psychiatry Emeritus at the State University of New York, Lifetime Fellow of the American Psychiatric Association and author of 23 books including his 1960 classic *The Myth of Mental Illness.* Dr. Szasz, an outspoken critic of his own profession, was not just talking about psychiatry in terms of the hospital and clinic, but the decline of our entire social structure. He added, "Psychiatry is a part of the general liberal ethos… everybody is a victim, everybody has special rights, no responsibility."[69]

Why would a man of such intellect as Thomas Szasz, a man of near-legendary status in his field, single out psychiatry as the most destructive force in America in the past fifty years? Szasz contends that while most have paid little attention, psychiatry has crept into schools, courtrooms, legislatures, workplace, and homes bringing with it psychological substitutes for virtue and individual responsibility.

Psychiatry's view of man and his problems has so infiltrated American thinking that people do not realize it is psychiatry. It is like the proverbial story of the frog and the kettle of water. Place a frog in boiling water and it will immediately jump out. Boiling water is a hostile environment. Place a frog in water that's room-temperature, a comfortable environment, he'll stay there. Even as the temperature of the water is slowly raised the frog, unaware his environment is changing, stays in the kettle. The frog is content. The water begins to boil. The frog boils too.

Most changes in society are *evolutionary* rather than *revolutionary.* The subtlety, the daily incremental shift in some aspect of life and thought, is disarming. The small and minute is dismissed while we stand guard against major assaults on our perspective of life. The single big bang we have steadfastly waited for is much smaller than the tiny cumulative changes that have become humongous, but unnoticed until now.

---

[69] *Ibid.*, p. 7.

Chapter 8
The Human Mind: Marvel of Creation

After thousands of scientists have studied the brain for centuries, the only adequate way to describe it is as a miracle.

Robert Ornstein / Richard F. Thompson
Our Brain —A Living Labyrinth

What is man that You take thought of him, and the son of man that You care for him? Yet You have made him a little lower than God, and You crown him with glory and majesty!

David
Psalm 8:4-5 NASU

God's miracle of creation is rivaled in Scripture only by the work He performed while Christ hung on the Cross of Calvary. In the beginning, God created. When we attempt to wrap our minds around this event where all was formed from nothingness, it boggles the human imagination. The very universe with all its wonders, galaxies, star systems, and mysteries contains so many inconceivable facts; no one on this earth can even begin to understand them. Science has attempted to explain away the marvels of God's creation, yet despite the advances man makes in a hundred scientific disciplines, we are just not able to explain it all fully. God created something from nothing and no amount of science can completely explain that phenomenon and its results.

The field of medicine is no different. Advances in understanding the human body, its structure and inner workings, have been marvelous, particularly over the past three hundred years. Through His general revelation, God has allowed us to discover, describe and demystify much of what makes us tick. Today we have medicines that cure, surgeries that heal, and physical therapies that rehabilitate. However, man has become arrogant as his perceived understanding of the universe has grown. The wonders and mysteries of God have been peeled away by what man believes to be irrefutable scientific evidence. Man has placed himself at the center of the universe and cast God aside as a myth. Worldviews are changing and man has become independent from his Creator.

Distinctive Creation [70]

What man does not understand, he attempts to explain through scientific means. Biological psychiatry would have us believe the biblical heart or mind of man is synonymous with the brain. Man does not possess a soul as he is simply a more highly evolved animal; thus all his feelings, behaviors, attitudes and thoughts are a result of chemical processes occurring within his brain. The genesis of this specific line of thinking began with the German philosopher Christian Wolff (1679-1754) and is known as monism, meaning oneness. Growing out of monism was a philosophy that attempted to explain everything in a singular unifying principle. Materialism, as it was called, denied the existence of God or anything supernatural and classified everything as a result of the interaction or properties of matter. It is found in the later writings of Freidrich Engels (1820-1895) who was the co-founder of what we know today as Marxism. Engels said, "The material world which can be observed by our senses, to which we ourselves belong, is the only reality...matter is not the result of mind, but mind is merely the highest product of matter." Engels dismissed all things supernatural and placed man at the center of the evolving universe. As a result, man is seen simply as a higher form of evolution and is fundamentally no different than a plant or an animal. He simply evolved differently.

Scripture differs significantly from this assertion beginning even prior to the creation of man. First, an unseen, immaterial God created the animals "after their (or its) kind" (Genesis 1:21, 24-25). However, in Genesis 1:26, God says, *"Let Us make man in Our image, according to Our likeness...."* In this simple statement, God decreed man to be different than all the rest of His creation. He is specifically saying

---

[70] For further study read A. Hoekema, *Created in God's Image.* (Grand Rapids, MI: Eerdmans Publishing Company 1986).

that man will be different from the animals He created. While the building blocks used to make His creatures are similar in that all living organisms possess DNA as their most basic construct, man would be different because of what God would do not to his body, but to his soul. How is man different? Consider these attributes of man and contrast them to animals:

- man is morally accountable before God
- man possesses an immaterial soul allowing communion with God as a Spirit,
- man possesses immortality in spirit
- man possesses the ability for abstract reasoning and logical thinking
- man possesses the use of complex, abstract language
- man possesses an awareness of the distant future
- man possesses creativity (art, music, theatre, etc.)
- man possesses a complexity of emotions
- man possesses deep interpersonal relationships
- man possesses the right to rule over creation

God created man as both material (body) and immaterial (soul, heart, mind). Interestingly, it should also be noted that God created the plants and animals first and then "counsels" with all the members of the Godhead before making man. Surely, man is different.

If man is made in the image and likeness of God, what does this mean for you? Actually, the question is a much bigger one. The question is that of creature and Creator. As Christians, we hold that God is the Creator and man is but one of His creations. In fact, looking around us, everything our senses can perceive has been created. Our entire reality is a product of God's creative nature. As such, man does not live independently from God. Even the man shipwrecked on a deserted island for scores of years lives dependently upon his Creator. We are all (believers and unbelievers alike) dependent upon Him for *everything*. He provides basics such as warmth, light, gravity, air, protection from cosmic forces, rain, materials for shelter, food…and the list goes on and on. We would call that common grace as the sun shines and the rain falls on both the just as well as the unjust (Matthew 5:45). Does this then mean man is simply a celestial puppet, dangled on God's string for His pleasure? No. It does not. God has also created man to be a person with a certain level of independence. Man can make his own choices within the realm of options offered to him.

For example, a man may choose to fly. He may do so in a variety of ways from hang-gliders to jumbo jets but he cannot step off a 10-story building and expect to mount the wind like a comic book super-hero. He may choose how to fly, but that choice must be within a certain realm of realistic options based on God's order of the universe.

Therefore, man is both a creature and a person, an intermingling of material and immaterial. How can he be both? How can he be absolutely dependent upon God and yet be independent in decision making? Dependence and freedom are a paradox. Scripture says in Romans 9:21, *"Or does not the potter have a right over the clay, to make from the same lump one vessel for honorable use and another for common use?"* Yet in Galatians 6:7-8, Paul says, *"Do not be deceived, God is not mocked; for whatever a man sows, this he will also reap. For the one who sows to his own flesh will from the flesh reap corruption, but the one who sows to the Spirit will from the Spirit reap eternal life."* Rational human minds cannot resolve this perceived contradiction, yet this is what Scripture teaches. For man to deny either side leads him into error. Hence, man must rely on faith to settle the argument. Faith is an attribute not shared by plants or even animals. Faith is a product of being made in the image and likeness of God.

In order for man to know God, God must regenerate him, giving him a renewed heart. At the same time, the man must make a personal choice to accept Christ and to follow Him as both Lord and Savior. To further complicate the issue, God is the one who gives man the ability to make the choice for Christ. Left to himself, man would never come to Christ of his own free choice. Because man is so gripped by his sinful nature, only God can set him free. All of this is possible through man's creation in the image and likeness of God. But again, man is bound to choose and operate according to God's natural laws. As a result of the Fall, man is completely unable to choose God freely. God must work a regenerative miracle for man to possess the ability to choose Christ. This miracle would be impossible but for the fact that man is indeed made in God's image and likeness.

To what, exactly, does the image of God in man need to be restored? If Scripture does not tell us, how can we know? It is not the ability to reason nor is it the ability to make choices. The image and likeness of God is manifest in Christ who is the image of God as God. It is Jesus we should emulate. His qualities should penetrate our very being as we are sanctified or changed into His image. We can know what we need to be restored to by observing the perfect God-man Jesus Christ. According to Colossians 3:14, we can see one attribute standing above the rest binding them all together: *Beyond all these things put on love, which is the perfect bond of unity.* No one up to the time of Christ, and no one since has exhibited the kind of love He exhibited. He loved His fellow man and He loved God. As the one who was totally without sin, He lived as the image and likeness of God. If we want to see what we are missing, so to speak, we need look no further for comparison than to view the life of Christ. How then, do we strive to achieve Christ-likeness? As we are told in Ephesians 4, we must put off the old man, renew the spirit of our minds, and put on the new man. We must change the old, habitual unrighteousness and retrain our brains and bodies to think and behave righteously.

Material Man

The human brain functions on a level medical science does not even begin to understand. Despite all of the theories, the human brain is as vast as the universe itself and is understood at only a very basic, rudimentary level. Medical science cannot explain it, physical science cannot quantify it and philosophy can only muse over it. The human brain is a remarkable creation, not honed over billions of years of natural selection and evolution, but created by a Being who is Himself beyond complete understanding. Yet despite its vastness, something is missing. The brain simply functions as the receiver of information in the physical world. Due to the effects of the fall, it no longer possesses the full complement of analytical capabilities as it was intended originally.

Moreover, the brain is only part of the human experience. When we attempt to alter the function of a human brain with external chemicals in order to control behavior, we are sailing into uncharted territory. We have not even begun to understand the nuances and intricacies of the brain's function. We do not fully understand the nature or scope of drug therapy on the brain or other physical organs and we do not fully understand the link between the brain, the drugs, and behavior. More sobering as Christians is our limited view of how the brain, indistinguishable from the body scripturally, differs from the heart, soul, and a variety of other terms the Bible uses to describe that which is immaterial in man.

The brain is included within the Scriptural term "soma", meaning the body itself, which we experience with our senses and often associate with a person. It is also included in the Old Testament term "basar" (Numbers 16:22) and its New Testament equivalent, "sarx" (II Peter 2:17-19), which refers to flesh. Flesh is the living tissue of the body, referring to its composition. In addition, flesh often relates to sinful weakness or that which renders us incapable of doing what is right according to Scripture. However, contrary to some early teaching around the church (Gnosticism, Doceticism, Cerinthianism), the body in and of itself is not evil. The body is matter and all matter was created by God. He refers to it as being good. Thus, the body is respected in Scripture as something good. On the other hand, the body affected by sin is evil because it does not function as it was intended in the worship of and reverence for the Creator. The results of the Fall, sin and death, affect both the immaterial or spiritual man and subsequently his material body. The hosts of organic, physiological problems, known collectively as diseases, are inherent in this fallen physical body. Legitimate medicine functions to address these diseases therapeutically.

Something astounding happens in the believer, however, at the point of regeneration. We change.

> **Or do you not know that your body is a temple of the Holy Spirit who is in you, whom you have from God, and that you are not your own? For you have been bought with a price: therefore glorify God in your body** (I Corinthians 6:19-20).

Regeneration changes many things; both material and spiritual (see below). Materially, the body is "purchased" and no longer belongs to itself. The body becomes the tool or avenue through which the Christian glorifies God through the outflowing of the Holy Spirit. The Christian becomes a slave to God, no longer directing his own path, but following the path set forth by his new Master. The body, including the brain, whose actions and thoughts are consumed by sin, at regeneration, has the capacity to be reprogrammed against habitual sinfulness. Christian man has once again been given the ability to choose good over evil (as in Adam). He has a renewed capacity to be righteous. This is a restorative change brought about instantaneously by the power of the Holy Spirit to God's elect. If this were the end of the story, we could all pack up and go home to Eden. But there is more.

The devil is a powerful master and he will not relinquish his children without an ongoing fight. Despite having lost yet another soul to the glory of God, the enemy is still *indirectly* active in the remnant habits left behind in the body. While the Christian is regenerated both materially and spiritually, he can and often does still sin. Every Christian can give personal testimony of the things they intend to do for God, but find their flesh in the way. Paul, in Romans 7:14-25, discusses this very issue. The sinful heart has programmed the flesh to act and react in a prescribed manner. Writing a new process over the old takes time and effort and is outlined clearly in Scripture.

Most troublesome, but entirely predictable, is the failure of the scientific community to recognize the biblical heart as the missing component of the complete human experience. The spiritual or immaterial heart is the interface between the physiologic brain of the natural world and the richness of the supernatural world. In order to effect change on a permanent basis in the believer, a spiritual component is required. God changes a man by changing the immaterial as change is a function of the heart. This is what the materialist denies and why secular theories on change (counseling) are ineffective. These secular theories rely on unproven chemical imbalances as causes and drugs whose action we do not fully understand as cures.[71] Materialistic diagnoses rule and Christian people are deceived.

Immaterial Man

Whereas the brain is the material receiver of data in the empirical, physical world, the "heart" is the evaluator of that world's data. The heart gives man the ability to turn data into information, thus the heart enables man to form worldviews and presuppositions. To the materialist, the notion of a supernatural component of man is foolishness, though this too is spoken of in Scripture.

> **For the word of the cross is foolishness to those who are perishing, but to us who are being saved it is the power of God. For it is written, "I WILL DESTROY THE WISDOM OF THE WISE, AND THE CLEVERNESS OF THE CLEVER I WILL SET ASIDE." Where is the wise man? Where is the scribe?**

---

[71] For a more detailed discussion on the chemical imbalance theory of Biological Psychiatry see *Deceptive Diagnosis: When Sin Is Called Sickness* by David Tyler and Kurt Grady, Focus Publishing, Bemidji, MN.

> Where is the debater of this age? Has not God made
> foolish the wisdom of the world? For since in the
> wisdom of God the world through its wisdom did not
> come to know God, God was well-pleased through
> the foolishness of the message preached to save
> those who believe. For indeed Jews ask for signs
> and Greeks search for wisdom; but we preach Christ
> crucified, to Jews a stumbling block and to Gentiles
> foolishness, but to those who are the called, both
> Jews and Greeks, Christ the power of God and the
> wisdom of God. Because the foolishness of God is
> wiser than men, and the weakness of God is stronger
> than men (I Corinthians 1:18-21).

At the core of the debate between the materialists and Christianity is the issue of worldview and the presuppositions brought to bear in determining that worldview. The materialist and the evolutionist are similar in their views as opposed to the Christian. The former groups discount a spiritual aspect of man, while the latter believes with all hope in such.

There are a number of descriptors of immaterial man used in Scripture, both in the Old and in the New Testament. Translated, these are words such as heart, soul, spirit, and mind. Each word speaks of the same general principle, the immaterial, though they are each different in their application. The immaterial heart is the inner you. It is the part of you that no one sees except you and God. It is the internal life that directs thinking, acting, behaving, willing, remembering and reasoning.

> But the things that proceed out of the mouth come
> from the heart, and those defile the man. For out of
> the heart come evil thoughts, murders, adulteries,
> fornications, thefts, false witness, slanders (Matthew
> 15:18-19).

> Watch over your heart with all diligence, for from it
> flow the springs of life (Proverbs 4:23).

Every bit of our lives pours out of the heart, and in the unregenerate man, that which pours out is sinful through and through. In the new man, the heart is the wellspring of a life lived for Christ. Spirit is that part of you in the absence of a body. Jesus said, "See My hands and My feet, that it is I Myself; touch Me and see, for a spirit does not have flesh and bones as you see that I have." (Luke 24:39). God the Father does not have a physical body and He is referred to as a Spirit. The third member of the tri-unity of God also exists as a Spirit. God is never referred to as a "soul" and we never see the Holy Spirit referred to as the Holy Soul. "God is spirit, and those who worship Him must worship in spirit and truth" (John 4:23). Thus, by definition soul and spirit are different. At the same time, however, they are the same because soul refers to the spirit when it is united with the body. "And the LORD God formed man of the dust of the ground, and breathed into his nostrils the breath of life; and man became a living soul" (Genesis 2:7 KJV).

The soul is the same immaterial part of you as the spirit and the heart, yet it refers to the immaterial joined to the material. Spirit, soul and heart refer to the same consciousness in different forms. Practically speaking, mind also refers to the immaterial you meaning the center of the consciousness or understanding. When joined with the body, mind is synonymous with soul and when absent from the body, it is the same as spirit. At Adam's creation, God made a body from the elements of the earth and then filled it with life. It was that uniting of spirit with body that resulted in a man with a material body and a mind, heart or soul. Prior to that breath of life, man was just a dead, mindless collection of raw materials (dust). When life entered, so did mind. Mind is a product of spirit, not of body and not of brain.

Hence, man is *duplexity*. He is material and immaterial folded together in order to make up a complete person. Some use the term dichotomy (meaning to cut in two), though this more accurately describes what occurs at death when the soul and the body are separated or "dichotomized" into a lifeless body of flesh and a living spirit.[72] "For just as the body without the spirit is dead..." (James 2:26).

The heart is the seat of the consciousness of man. It gives man the ability to perceive and to think even when it exists outside the body (consider the experiences of the Apostles John - (Revelation 1:10) and Paul - II Corinthians 12:2-4). The regenerated heart restores man to his original construct in the image and likeness of God and, as a result, gives him the ability to commune with his Creator. In modern day wisdom, the heart is a myth of an all but dead religion. Psychology

---

[72] Jay E. Adams, *The Biblical Perspective on the Mind-Body Problem*, Part One. *Journal of Biblical Ethics in Medicine*. Vol. 7 (2): pp. 15-24 and Vol. 7 (3): pp. 1-10.

and psychiatry claim to have the answers, but in over one hundred years of collective psychological practice, our world is spiraling further and further out of control. It is getting worse and not better. People today are consumed as never before with so-called mental problems. In reality, the heart is the key to understanding man and his thinking and behavior. God has always had the answers to the questions man has been asking and He has provided those in a handy collection of wisdom called the Bible. The Bible explains the heart in detail and we would be well served by mining its wisdom and applying its solutions to hearts in need of change. A biblically changed heart leads to changes in physiology, personality, and behavior. All the psychological theory to date and henceforth to the Rapture will never grasp the absolute necessity for Christ in effecting true, lasting change.

The Whole Man

Though we have explored the material brain (body) and the immaterial heart (heart, mind, soul) as separate and distinct entities, they are, in many ways, interconnected and intertwined. That which affects the heart affects the brain and that which affects the brain can, in turn, affect the heart. It is this heart/brain complex that must be addressed in order to affect lasting change. The materialist denies the existence of the heart and only addresses the brain. This is the approach of biological psychiatry. All behavior is *"thought to"* be the result of the chemical interactions between the various nerve cells in the brain. The Christian is different because of his regeneration. Man, outside of fellowship with God, is incomplete so the changing power of regeneration restores fellowship and the ability to commune with God. The change God commands of those who are His is referred to as sanctification and it is, in essence, replacing the thoughts and behavior of the god of this world with the thoughts and behavior of Christ.

In the unregenerate, the heart is hopelessly sinful and oriented toward evil, just like that of Satan. Thoughts and behaviors are unrighteous because of the orientation of the heart. The heart controls the body and what flows from the unregenerate heart, by definition, cannot be good in the sight of God. Can unregenerate man do "good" deeds? Of course he can. However, in Isaiah, the so-called good works of the unrighteous are likened to filthy rags to God. Unregenerate man can do nothing to merit God's favor. Likewise, in the Christian, good done in our own power is of no value to God. It is the good the regenerate do in the power of Christ that God favors. Regeneration is what allows the power of Christ to begin the change process in man. It is what makes the difference in the ability to make lasting change.

Consider the analogy of sight. Unregenerate man can see, though it is as if he can only see out of one eye. Something is missing in his monocular vision. The data being fed into the brain through the optic nerve is limited and unnatural because the body is designed to receive input from two eyes. In the analogy, regeneration restores that which is missing. With two eyes, binocular vision is restored. With binocular vision, man has considerably more information with which to work. The full amount of data is entering the brain via the two optic nerves. Depth perception is restored and all of the advantages of the way our eyes and brain were designed are restored. Similarly, upon regeneration, the heart of man is restored to function as it was originally designed. Man is now able to communicate with God as he was created to do in the Garden. Likewise, the Holy Spirit can communicate in a very intimate, personal way with man's restored heart. The heart is changed and, in turn, the brain follows suit as it is re-programmed with righteousness.

How the Heart affects the Brain

As the immaterial component of man, the heart is the ultimate precursor of thinking and behaving in man. Lasting change in these areas of behavior must come first through a change in the heart and then a retraining or reprogramming of the brain. The physical organ becomes habituated to certain thoughts and behaviors mediated by the heart. As the heart changes, so the brain changes also. In some people, upon regeneration, changes in thinking and behavior occur immediately. The drunkard no longer has a taste for alcohol or the angry man is transformed into a meek and humble individual. In most, however, changing our sinful habituations is a difficult, frustrating and lifelong endeavor.

Those who have difficulty making the changes dictated by a life in Christ need to seek a Scriptural solution to the change process. Scripture is the prescription written by the Great Physician. Scripture outlines, in detail, how we are to change. We are to *put off the old, put on the new all while renewing the mind.* Ephesians 4 and Colossians 3 offer a detailed description and chapter five, "ADHD: The Biblical

Diagnosis", contains a practical application of these verses. In short, the heart is renewed by the Word of God as the Christian puts off the old thinking and behavior and retrains or rehabituates the brain to put on habitually righteous thinking and behavior. The changed heart leads to a changed brain. The immaterial directly affects the material.

How the Brain affects the Heart

It is somewhat easy to see how the heart affects the brain when we think about it from a Scriptural perspective. However, it is more difficult to understand how the brain affects the heart. How can the material affect the immaterial? Have we not stated that the heart is the seat of consciousness giving one the ability to think and perceive through the activity of the brain? How could a tool (brain) affect the operator (heart)? Remember that the brain is the sensory input device for the body. In order for the heart to make decisions, it needs information fed through the senses. Anything that affects the brain's ability to deliver information affects the heart's ability to make appropriate decisions. For example, consider the affect hearing loss has on adults. Their ability to determine what is going on around them is severely hampered. We have all experienced individuals who have become inwardly focused, angry and bitter as a result of feeling excluded. The lack of information entering the brain as a result of damaged nerves in the ear has affected the heart by limiting input. A similar situation could occur as a person experiences a loss of eyesight. Anything that limits the ability for the heart to obtain full information needed to make decisions is an indirect affect by the body on the heart. Organic diseases such as tumors and Alzheimer's and other forms of dementia can also affect the heart by limiting the way information is processed and delivered for consideration by the heart. Likewise, and most pertinent to this book is the question of how drugs can affect the heart of man.

How do drugs affect the brain and the heart?

From substantial amounts of animal data and years of observation, we can be reasonably certain drugs affect the brain causing a wide variety of responses in thinking and behavior. However, to date, medical science has not been able to explain exactly how any so-called mental health drugs actually work. Because they do seem to work, it is easy to understand the alleged connection between drugs and brain. Antidepressants can lift mood. Anxiolytics can reduce anxiety. Antipsychotics can reduce bizarre thoughts and focus erratic thinking. Do drugs correct alleged chemical imbalances that cause unwanted thoughts and behavior? No. It is clear from the previous discussion that thoughts are rooted in the heart and not the brain. Drugs only provide a measure of symptom relief and not lasting change. The drugs affect the material part of man, not the immaterial. There is no such thing as a pill to cure the curse of sin on the heart. Through trial and error, we have determined that certain drugs seem to alleviate the symptoms of some problems. We do not know why or how, but we know they do.

If the drugs affect the brain, which they appear to do, they have the ability to affect the heart by changing how the brain receives and processes information. For example, drugs used in the treatment of anxiety disorders often leave people feeling detached or "zoned out". Are they effective for treating the anxiety? Yes. However, consider the cost. The fact that the drugs reduce anxiety is but a secondary effect to that fact that the senses are blunted into a near-euphoric "buzz". The brain is affected to such a degree as to limit the amount of information reaching the heart. Whatever issue was at the root of the anxiety is dulled and that is the objective of the therapy. Problems have not been solved, rather they have been anesthetized. In order to keep the problems from returning, the drug must be continued. The same is true for the drugs given for ADHD. The child's behavior and thinking is slowed. Externally, the child appears to be much calmer and pliable, when, in fact they are blunted into a relative stupor. The objectives of a calmer home or classroom are met while the child withdraws into a world of a false existence. Their thinking has not changed, as is evidenced by the return of their behavior once the drugs are discontinued. All that has been addressed is the effect they are having on others who are dissatisfied with how the child interacts with his world.

Medication is not the answer for non-organic problems of living. Changing to become more like Christ each day is the prescription to be taken and applied liberally in individuals and families as opposed to taking a drug for every untoward behavior. Man's separation from God is the problem and Jesus Christ is the solution.

What is all the fuss with heart and brain about? This is the crux of the argument. This is what must be mastered in order to understand change. Change is not exclusively behavioral or exclusively brain-centered. Change is spiritual. Change in position before God occurs spiritually through regeneration and specifically justification. The heart, separated from God, has programmed the body to respond habitually to certain stimuli. In order to change, the heart must reprogram the brain to function differently. For the heart to reprogram the brain in a way that will allow the body to edify the Creator, the heart must be reconnected to the Creator through regeneration. This is the process whereby the image and likeness of God is restored in fallen man allowing him to once again choose good over evil. If the heart is going to reprogram the brain to perform righteously, the heart must first become righteous.

Chapter 9
Amphetamine Anyone?

Ritalin™ has come to play the role of an overt instrument of social control.

Francis Fukuyama,
Our Posthuman Future

See to it that no one takes you captive through philosophy and empty deception, according to the tradition of men, according to the elementary principles of the world, rather than according to Christ.

Apostle Paul
Colossians 2:8

For many years, the mainstay in treating children with attention disorders has been the amphetamines and the amphetamine-like drugs. This "breakthrough" in medicine was discovered completely by accident in 1937. A physician in a home for children with behavioral and neurological problems experimented with amphetamine as a pain reliever for headaches resulting from spinal taps. He found there was little relief of headaches, but the children were markedly more docile and agreeable. He believed children had a different reaction to the amphetamines than adults which eventually led to the belief that children who responded to the amphetamines, sometimes in dramatic ways, must have some sort of hyperkinetic brain dysfunction or disorder that the drug addressed.

Yet another "breakthrough" occurred in 1944 when methylphenidate was synthesized at Ciba pharmaceuticals (now Novartis). Its pharmacology (i.e. how the drug works) was not described until 1954. The U.S. Food and Drug Administration (FDA) approved Ritalin® (methylphenidate) in 1961. By the early 1970's, there were about 150,000 children taking the drug. From this and other data, the terminology "minimal brain dysfunction" (MBD) was coined in place of the earlier term, hyperkinesis. Eventually, the FDA struck the MBD terminology as unscientific. However, the so-called condition was simply renamed Attention Deficit Disorder (ADD) and its criteria broadened considerably. ADD was first seen in the *Diagnostic and Statistical Manual of Mental Health Disorders* (DSM), Third Edition in 1980. Given the new broadening of criteria, millions of children could be included as "having" ADD. In 1987, with the release of a revised and updated DSM, the criteria was expanded even further with the emergence of a subtype of ADD known as attention deficit hyperactivity disorder or ADHD.

The pharmaceutical industry and others saw that physicians were duly informed of the dangers of ADD and ADHD and were thus encouraged to use drugs to combat the scourge of fidgetiness. In its ever-present greed, the pharmaceutical industry has recently been targeting adults for treatment for ADHD. Poor performance in college or at work or inattentiveness at home may be a resurgence of the childhood problem of an attention disorder. It is interesting to note how little we heard about adult attention deficit disorder when there was not a brand drug on the market to treat it. We began seeing and hearing more about this plague of modern adults just prior to Eli Lilly and Company's release of Strattera®, which is indicated in both children and in adults. Is it not interesting how so many new diseases are being discovered just prior to the launch of a new drug which can be used to treat it? While the drug companies are creating so-called diseases to treat with their newest drugs, the world is still dealing with AIDS, cancer, heart disease, killer bacteria and viruses, and a host of other real diseases. Then again, it is a lot harder to cure a documented disease than it is to create one to fit a drug already in the company's pipeline.

Today, the use of the ADHD drugs is supported based on their *theoretical* impact on the *proposed* chemical imbalances of attention disorders. Other agents have been studied (clonidine and guanfacine) based on their molecular similarity to amphetamine and many other drugs and brands have entered the lucrative market. (See table 1 for a complete listing of the amphetamines and amphetamine-like drugs available in the United States for ADHD). There is one agent, atomoxetine, originally cast as an anti-depressant, which has been found to have effectiveness in treating ADHD. The link between antidepressants, particularly the newer selective serotonin re-uptake inhibitors (i.e. Prozac®, Paxil®, Zoloft®, Luvox®, Cymbalta®, Celexa®, Lexapro®, Pristig®) and the amphetamines is significant and will be briefly explored below.

A Foundation on Amphetamine

The amphetamine class of drugs belongs to a larger group know as the sympathomimetics (sim-path-o-my-met-ics). The sympathomimetics have wide and varying actions in the body and affect most organ systems in some way. Several drugs commonly used in both hospitals and in the community are sympathomimetics. Some of these include epinephrine (for severe allergic reactions or cardiac arrest), dopamine (to increase blood pressure and kidney function), dobutamine (to improve heart pumping), ritodrine (to reduce uterine contractions in premature labor), and albuterol (to improve breathing). The mechanism of action of these drugs is well understood and can be consistently demonstrated in both animals and in humans.

The amphetamines are in a subclass of sympathomimetics known as the adrenergic agonists, meaning they have powerful stimulatory effects on the central nervous system (CNS). How the amphetamines exert their effect throughout the CNS, according to *Goodman & Gillman's The Pharmacological Basis of Therapeutics, 10th Edition*, widely accepted as the authoritative reference book in pharmacology, is clearly up for debate, given the number of "hedge words"[73] used (in bold).

> These effects are **thought to** be due to cortical stimulation and **possibly** to stimulation of the reticular activating system...**appears to** exert **most or all** of its effects in the CNS by releasing biogenic amines from their storage sites in nerve terminals...**presumably** mediated by the release of norepinephrine...**probably** are a consequence of the release of dopamine...**may** be due to a release of 5-hydroxytryptamine...**may** exert direct effects on central receptors...[74](emphasis ours)

They also cause appetite suppression, nasal decongestion, increased blood pressure, decreased or increased heart rate, and dilation of lung bronchi. Sometimes they cause an irregular heart

---

[73] "Hedge words" is a phrase coined by the author (Grady) to illustrate words that are often overlooked but that speak volumes. These are words the scientific community likes to use in the midst of very technical jargon that communicate the fact that this is an educated best guess, but not conclusive scientific truth. Thus, though complex and technical in description, some words are inserted allowing for "hedging"...

[74] JG Hardman, LE Limbird eds., *Goodman & Gillman's The Pharmacologic Basis of Therapeutics, Tenth Edition.* (New York, NY: McGraw-Hill Medical Publishing Division, 2001), pp. 235, 236.

beat. Difficulty in urination can occur due to effects on the smooth muscle in the bladder. It is important to understand that the effects and side effects of the amphetamines can occur *at any dose*, regardless of whether or not the dose is considered within the "normal" range.

The CNS effects differ from person to person and based upon the dose given. At "normal" doses, an individual is likely to experience wakefulness, alertness, decreased sense of fatigue, mood elevation, increased initiative, self-confidence, increased ability to concentrate, elation, euphoria, and increased motor and speech activities. However, there is a price to be paid for what seems to be quite beneficial. Though more work may be accomplished in a given period of time, errors are more frequent. Over time, larger doses are needed to cause the same effects. This is a phenomenon known as tolerance. As doses increase, so do unwanted side effects. Depression and fatigue are common along with headache, heart palpitations, dizziness, irritability, confusion, apprehension, and delirium. Sleep disturbances are common and it may take as long as *two months* for sleep patterns to return to normal after the drugs are discontinued. With even higher doses, sensory perception is altered and psychotic behavior can result. Paranoid hallucinations are common as doses increase. As with the mechanism of action of the drugs themselves, how or why these side effects occur and specifically at what doses is not completely understood. Significant "person-to-person" variability occurs.

Other side effects commonly seen include restlessness, tremor, hyperactive reflexes, talkativeness, tenseness, insomnia, fever, aggressiveness, changes in libido, anxiety, panic states, suicidal or homicidal tendencies (especially in those with other "mental disorders"), flushing, chest pain, high or low blood pressure, sweating, dry mouth, metallic taste, nausea, vomiting, diarrhea, stomach cramping, and seizures. The doses required to cause these effects vary widely from one person to another meaning that one dose may be fine for one person while that same dose could cause significant problems in someone else.

In looking back at the amphetamine's proposed mechanism of action on various organ systems in the body, note the number of times a definitive answer is NOT given. Hedge words like *"thought to, appears, may, probably, presumably"* occur throughout leading one to conclude that we really do know how these drugs work. In fact, no drug used in the treatment of attention disorders or any other "mental disorder" holds a definitive mechanism of action.

If we examined the FDA approved package labeling (package insert) for the antidepressants, anti-anxiety drugs, drugs for bipolar disorder, drugs for attention disorders, drugs for schizophrenia and a host of others, we would not find a single case where science has explained how the drug works in the particular condition for which it is indicated. In part, this comes from the fact that no data exists to support the biological basis for the presence of a chemical imbalance or a disease. If no pathology of the tissue can be identified, it is no wonder we have no idea how the drugs work. We know they work in some people, and we have drawn our scientific conclusions from faulty logic. Just because the drugs may affect chemicals in the brain, we have concluded there is a chemical imbalance simply because the drugs seem to work in some people. Unfortunately, this level of drug experimentation is being carried out on millions of children each and every day.[75]

Dependence is an issue as well with the amphetamines. Tolerance to the beneficial effects occur necessitating increasing dosages in order to achieve the same clinical effect.[76] One needs look no further for evidence of dependence, or addiction, than the middle United States, where the production of illicit methamphetamine is a significant problem for law enforcement and society at-large. New federal laws controlling the sale of the cold medicine pseudoephedrine (a chemical precursor of methamphetamine) have recently been enacted in an attempt to stem the "crystal meth" epidemic. In addition, each of the prescription amphetamines carries a boxed warning (the strongest warning Food and Drug Administration issues) cautioning physicians of the high abuse potential. In pharmacies, strict laws regarding the ordering, storage and dispensing of these medications are in place. The amphetamines are in the class of drugs known as Schedule II medications and their purchase is tracked to the very last tablet by the federal Drug Enforcement Agency and the state Bureaus of Narcotics and Dangerous Drugs. These are dangerously addictive drugs and this fact has been recognized for many years. However, parents of children labeled ADHD are often told the drugs are mild and possess few side effects or risks.

---

[75] For a more complete discussion of chemical imbalance theories in biological psychiatry, see *Deceptive Diagnosis: When Sin Is Called Sickness* by David Tyler and Kurt Grady (Focus Publishing, Bemidji, MN.).

[76] Interestingly, no tolerance or dosage escalation occurs in the treatment of narcolepsy (excessive daytime sleepiness) for which the amphetamines are legitimately prescribed.

Scientific Evidence

As with any drug, pharmacologists and other medical scientists are interested in knowing how the drugs cause their effects in the body. For example, we know how penicillin works in killing bacteria. Science has identified a binding protein on the cell wall of bacteria that, in the presence of penicillin, causes the cell wall to burst open, thus killing the bacteria. In asthmatics, inhaled beta-agonist drugs, like albuterol, bind to receptors on smooth muscle cells in the lungs causing muscle relaxation and an opening up of lung bronchi so patients can breathe more effectively. There is documented scientific evidence for both the conditions (infection, asthma) as well as the drug effects. The scientific evidence is proven in the test tube as well as in animals and in humans.

This is not the case for the amphetamines and amphetamine-like drugs used in the treatment of attention disorders. The Food and Drug Administration (FDA) package labeling for amphetamine says this regarding the use of these drugs in the treatment of attention disorders:

> There is **neither specific evidence** which clearly establishes the mechanism whereby amphetamine produces mental and behavioral effects in children, **nor conclusive evidence** regarding how these effects relate to the condition of the central nervous system.[77]

There is similar language for the mixed salts of dextroamphetamine [®][78] (Adderall XR®):

> **The mode of therapeutic action in Attention Deficit Hyperactivity Disorder is not known.** Amphetamines are **thought to** block the reuptake of norepinephrine and dopamine into the presynaptic neuron and increase the release of these monoamines into the extraneuronal space.[79] (emphasis ours).

---

[77] Package Labeling, Amphetamine/Dextroamphetamine Mixed Salts, (Pomona, NY: Barr Laboratories, August, 2005). (emphasis mine)

[78] [⊥] Mixed salts of dextroamphetamine was once marketed under the name Obetrol and was used primarily in women to promote weight loss. It was withdrawn from the market in 1981 due to a high addiction liability.

[79] Package Labeling, Adderall XR®, DSM Pharmaceuticals, (Greenville, NC: October, 2002). (emphasis mine)

In methylphenidate (Metadate CD®, Ritalin®, others) the most prescribed molecule for the treatment of attention disorders, the label reads:

> Methylphenidate HCl is a central nervous system (CNS) stimulant. **The mode of therapeutic action in Attention Deficit Hyperactivity Disorder (ADHD) is not known.** Methylphenidate is **thought to** block the reuptake of norepinephrine and dopamine into the presynaptic neuron and increase the release of these monoamines into the extraneuronal space.[80] (emphasis ours).

Atomoxetine, or Strattera®, is the newest drug used in the treatment of attention disorders, and though it is not an amphetamine, it is structurally related to the amphetamines and to the selective serotonin reuptake inhibitors like fluoxetine (Prozac®). Atomoxetine is not a controlled substance. It is indicated for use in both children and adults who exhibit the symptoms of attention disorders and it was investigated for use in depression, though it does not have an indication for depression at this time. Its package labeling says this of its mechanism of action:

> *The precise mechanism by which atomoxetine produces its therapeutic effect in Attention Deficit/Hyperactivity Disorder (ADHD) is unknown, but it is thought to be related to selective inhibition of the pre-synaptic norepinephrine transporter, as determined in ex vivo[81] uptake and neurotransmitter depletion studies.[82](emphasis ours).*

Here again, we can observe the language where there is truly no definitive evidence for the way the drug is "thought to" work and is based on the chemical imbalance theories of biological psychiatry. There are a multitude of hedge words used, but no scientific truth.

---

[80] Package Labeling, Metadate CD®, Celltech Pharmaceuticals, (Rochester, NY: July, 2003). (emphasis mine)

[81] *Ex vivo* refers to the use of human tissue in the test tube or other laboratory-type study. It is contrasted with *in vivo*, which means within the living human body and *in vitro*, which indicates laboratory testing in general with either animal tissue or some other type of study without the use of living cells or tissue.

[82] Package Labeling, Strattera®, Eli Lilly and Company, Indianapolis, IN, December, 2004 (emphasis mine)

Also of interest is the fact that atomoxetine has been studied in large numbers of people suffering from depression. From a corporate point of view, this makes good business sense. As stated above, atomoxetine is structurally related to fluoxetine (Prozac®) and they are both related to amphetamine. Fluoxetine began as a drug for weight loss due to it's similarity to amphetamine, though it did not perform well enough to warrant marketing. It did, however, seem to lift mood (as does amphetamine). Thus began the Prozac® era. Of note, amphetamines have also been studied in mild to moderate depression and have a history of use dating back into the late 1930's. It was effective in the kinds of depression that are treated today in the outpatient setting and is equally as effective as the newer SSRI antidepressants mentioned earlier. It is no wonder a drug (fluoxetine or atomoxetine) would be at least minimally effective in treating mild to moderate (outpatient) depression given its similarity to amphetamine. So, all of the marketing hoopla around the new class of antidepressants we experienced in the late 1980's and that is still going on today, was and is simply a repackaging of what we already knew minus the stigma of coming out and saying. "this is related to amphetamine."

Atomoxetine (Strattera®), being so similar to fluoxetine (Prozac®), also exhibits some limited weight loss properties and is also related to amphetamine. It was studied in over 1200 patients with depression, though, to date, it has not received an FDA indication for the treatment of depression. Atomoxetine is so similar to fluoxetine that they even share a similar side effect profile. Due to several post-marketing reports of suicide in children and teens taking SSRI antidepressants, the package labeling warnings about suicide in children and teens has been strengthened. The FDA now requires additional educational material to be dispensed with the antidepressant drugs when they are prescribed in this special population. There are four main points in the medication guide:

1. There is a risk of suicidal thoughts or actions

2. How to try to prevent suicidal thoughts or actions in your child

3. You should watch for certain signs if your child is taking an anti-depressant

4. There are benefits and risks when using anti-depressants

Each of these is further discussed in the medication guide.

Atomoxetine, the drug marketed only for ADHD and so structurally similar to the SSRI's, shares the suicide warning. Suicidal ideation (thoughts of committing suicide) was reported in clinical trials of atomoxetine.

The Bottom Line

The bottom line in exploring the drugs used in the treatment of attention disorders is this:

- We do not know how the drugs work
- The drugs have not been studied for a duration longer than 14 <u>weeks</u> though many children remain on them for decades
- We do know they "work" in some children making them more docile (acceptable to the teacher) in the classroom
- Some children have a spectrum of side effects from the mild to the severe; most children have at least some side-effect problems
- Some children have severe and sometimes violent reactions to these drugs
    - physicians sometimes mistake this behavior as being related to a subtherapeutic effect of the drugs and increase the dosage rather than discontinue the medication
    - as behavior worsens, more drugs are added in an experimental fashion
- Some children have died as a result of side effects

In the following chapters, we will address the evidence for attention disorders as a disease and we will then pool our conclusions.

Amphetamine, Brain and Heart

Hearkening back to the discussion about brain and heart, it is worth exploring exactly what is occurring in children who are medicated for their behavior. Biblically speaking, behavior flows from the heart. In translating what is "going on" in the heart, first, attitudes or thoughts are formed. Thereafter, those thoughts become feelings and actions or behaviors. Thoughts, feelings and behaviors are translated from the heart to the body by the brain. The heart affects the brain and thoughts, feelings and behaviors result. If we wish to affect behavior (i.e. ADHD) the brain is simply the intermediary carrying out the direction of the heart. The starting place in affecting behavior is not the brain, it is the heart. When we medicate the brain, we are affecting the intermediary and not the root cause of the behavior. Does behavior change in some? Yes. However, the heart is left unattended and the costs therein are immeasurable.

When the medication is tapered and discontinued, the behaviors return, sometimes worse than before. The habits ingrained within the heart are so well entrenched, when given the opportunity; they will emerge and manifest themselves in outward behavior. So, it could be argued that we should simply keep the medications going indefinitely. This approach would stifle the unwanted behavior permanently. This is exactly what the ADHD establishment, including the makers of ADHD drugs, want us to conclude. It keeps the child and even the adult ensnared in the mental health machine and enslaved to the pharmaceuticals. It means a steady supply of patients and prescriptions and thus a steady stream of money.

It also means we are not solving problems of living in a biblically faithful manner. Sanctification is halted and any hope of tangible spiritual growth is dashed against the curb at the pharmacy. The heart, designed to be changed in the believer, is left to percolate miserably in its own inherent sinfulness. Over time, that sinfulness will manifest itself in other ways, often making the fidgetiness of ADHD seem minor. The unrepentant heart is characterized in Jeremiah 17:9: "The heart is more deceitful than all else and is desperately sick; who can understand it?" The repentant heart is conversely seen characterized by Matthew 5:8: "Blessed are the pure in heart, for they shall see God."

The answer is to affect a change in heart, not simply a change in the flesh (brain). This has been God's plan from the beginning and one in which we would do well to avoid circumventing.

Generic Name	Trade Name(s)™	Dosage Form	Available Strengths
Methylphenidate	Ritalin®, Methylin®	Oral Tablets, Chewable Oral Tablets, Oral Solution	2.5mg, 5mg, 10mg, 20mg, 1mg/ml, 2mg/ml
Methylphenidate Extended (and Sustained) release	Ritalin SR®, Ritalin LA®, Concerta®, Metadate ER®, Metadate CD®	Oral Sustained and Extended-release Tablets and Capsules	10mg, 18mg, 20mg, 27mg, 30mg, 36mg, 40mg, 54mg
Methylphenidate transdermal patch	Daytrana®	Transdermal patch	10mg, 15mg, 20mg, 30mg
Dexmethylphenidate	Focalin®	Oral Tablets	2.5mg, 5mg, 10mg
Dexmethylphenidate Extended Release	Focalin XR®	Oral Extended-release Capsules	5mg, 10mg, 15mg, 20mg
Amphetamine/ Dextro-Amphetamine Mixed Salts	Adderall®	Oral Tablets	5mg, 10mg, 15mg, 20mg, 30mg
Amphetamine Extended Release	Adderall XR®	Extended–release oral capsules	5mg, 10mg, 15mg, 20mg, 25mg, 30mg
Dextroamphetamine	Dexedrine®, Dextrostat®	Oral tablets	5mg, 10mg
Dextroamphetamine Sustained release	Dexedrine Spansules®	Sustained-release oral capsules	5mg, 10mg, 15mg
Methamphetamine	Desoxyn®	Oral Tablets	5mg
Atomoxetine	Strattera	Oral capsules	10mg, 18mg, 25mg, 40mg, 60mg, 80mg, 100mg

Chapter 10
~~Informed~~ *"Conformed"* Consent

"Stephanie Hall was a fun-loving, outdoorsy girl with a joy for life who tried to make butterflies and ladybugs her pets...Stephanie Hall lived from January 11, 1984, until January 5, 1996 dying the morning after her Ritalin® dosage was upped, a drug she had been taking for five years, beginning soon after her school initiated the process of having her diagnosed ADD."

Fred A. Baughman, Jr.
The ADHD Fraud: How Psychiatry
Makes "Patients" of Normal Children.

And do not be conformed to this world, but be transformed by the renewing of your mind, so that you may prove what the will of God is, that which is good and acceptable and perfect.

Apostle Paul
Romans 12:2

The power wielded by psychiatry in drugging children is formidable, yet almost silent to the public at-large. Not a weekday goes by in our country where some parent is told his child has a brain disease called ADHD and must be medicated. They are told the medications are "mild" and have few side effects. Unfortunately, most parents, due to their own trust or naiveté, accept what they are being told and have the prescription(s) filled without question. The blind faith in school officials, psychologists, and social workers as well as with counselors and physicians of every flavor has led to millions of children being placed on amphetamine-like drugs for their so-called brain disease. Some of those children do well, though most suffer some severe side effects. Tragically, some children suffer irreversible physical damage and a number of deaths have been reported, directly related to the drugs themselves. Even so, the parent who refuses to comply with the "recommendations" of the "professionals" is in for a battle that, if lost, could cost them substantial amounts of time and money and, ultimately, custody of their child.

The mental health industry possesses great power in conjunction with the State. Because our society has accepted the biological psychology model of thinking, behaving and feeling as unalterable truth, the courts have followed suit. A parent who refuses to have his child medicated is seen as harming the child because the child has a disease and the parent is not allowing it to be treated. More than a few parents have heard the implied threat in the school official's voice when they are told to make an appointment for the child to see one of the school's doctors or the school will have no choice but to contact social services. Parents are conforming out of blind trust or fear, and their children are suffering as a result. They are unknowingly giving their consent to give their child, their most precious gift from God, a drug whose effects science does not fully understand for a "disease" no one has been able to prove even exists.

Informed consent is a "legal condition whereby a person can be said to have given consent based upon an appreciation and understanding of the facts and implications of an action."[83] Informed consent assumes the person is in a state of mind where he can reasonably understand the facts being presented to him. Children; those who are mentally retarded or mentally ill; those whose judgment is impaired by a disease (tumors or dementia, for example), drug or other substance or condition are not considered capable of giving informed consent. In most cases, if a person is unable to give consent, another person or authority is able to give consent on their behalf. Parents give consent for children, for example. The courts can give consent and, in the absence of such an authority in an emergency, health care practitioners work under implied consent in rendering life-saving care.

Consent is not as "cut-and-dried" as it may seem. People may give consent externally without appreciating all of the issues internally. Said another way, people say yes even though they do not fully understand what they are hearing or they have not had time to think it through considering all of the future implications or consequences.

---

[83] Wikipedia On-Line Encyclopedia at www.wikipedia.com

Consent may be given out of fear, social pressure, family pressure, or institutional pressure even though the individual is not fully informed. This is so much of a concern for the medical profession, written consent is often required before a procedure, surgery, or other invasive therapy is initiated. Legally, if a person signs a consent document, consent is given and all the facets of understanding are implied to be in place. In the United States of America, informed consent must communicate any significant risks upon which the patient may be exposed as a result of the therapy. Thus, informed consent assumes the patient (or guardian) is capable of making an informed decision specifically for themselves (or their charge).

Clearly we are not all medical professionals capable of understanding all of the technical aspects of surgeries and procedures. As such, the language used in informed consent documents and explanations must be general enough to be understandable by the lay person while being specific enough to truthfully convey the scope of the therapy as well as its risks. Medical institutions work very hard to be as explicit as possible without getting entangled in substantial technical terminology or the intricacies of what is being proposed. Good medical practice dictates the need for the physician to explain the therapy in detail, including its risks and benefits, in language the patient can easily understand, and answer any questions the patient may have.

Research Consent

In 1947, as a result of the gruesome human experiments of the Nazi's and in particular those of Dr. Josef Mengele and those of certain elements of the Japanese Army, a set of principles was set forth throughout the world to deal with the issue of human experimentation. The first document came out as a result of the Nuremberg war crimes trials and became known as the Nuremberg code. It was designed to be used as a guide in judging physicians and scientists who had conducted biomedical experiments on concentration camp prisoners. The ten points of the Nuremberg code are based on informed consent, absence of coercion, solid scientific methodologies, and a benefit for those participating in the experiments. We will list them later in this chapter.

Later, a set of ethical standards was adopted by the World Medical Association on the subject of human experimentation. The standards were completed in Helsinki, Finland in June, 1964 and have become known as the Declaration of Helsinki. Over time, the accord has been revised a number of times with the last update coming in 2000. Like the Nuremberg code, the Declaration of Helsinki places the issue of informed consent at the very top of the list. Moreover, the Declaration affirms that a research subject who is legally incompetent (i.e. a child), must agree to the decision to participate in the research in addition to that given by the legal guardian. What is also significant about the Declaration of Helsinki is that it was the first effort put forth by the medical community in an attempt to regulate itself.

In the United States in 1974, the National Research Act became law creating the National Commission for the Protection of Human Subjects of Biomedical and Behavioral Research. A charge of the commission was to identify basic ethical principles that should underlie this type of research and the result of that charge was the Belmont Report. It became a document which dictated the policies of the Federal Government's Department of Health and Human Services and is recorded in the Federal Register. The report contains three principles as well as a description of the distinction between research and practice and their application.

The distinction between research and practice is important in the discussion of treating children or adults who have been diagnosed with ADHD. *As medical science does not understand the so-called disease process in ADHD, its treatment may be considered experimental. Moreover, as medical science does not understand the action of the medications used in treating ADHD, the drug treatment should likewise be considered experimental.* Combined, we have a set of behaviors labeled as a disease where no one has been able to identify any brain abnormality being treated with a drug whose action no one really understands in humans. While millions of people have been "treated" with perhaps billions of doses of medication, it does not change the fact that we are still dealing with the unknown. An unknown "disease" being treated with drugs full of unknowns sounds like experimentation and should be treated as such.

In the Belmont Report, however, "practice" is defined by virtue of the improvement garnered by the individual through diagnosis, preventative treatment or therapy. Research is then defined as the testing of a hypothesis so that conclusions can be drawn and shared. A distinction must be made between "standard practice" and "proven practice" in order to support virtually every mental health diagnosis. There are few "proven" practices in mental health but there are many "standard" practices. In a way, standard practices are like some traditions in the church. While there is no biblical mandate for the traditions, many adhere to them as if there were. "We have always done it this way" trumps biblical truth because people are reluctant to change. Likewise, in mental health, there are many standard practices because "we have always done it this way" trumps proven science. Both are very pragmatic approaches. Certain traditions seem to work for some churches and if it works for us, why change? Similarly, certain drugs seem to help certain people who are exhibiting certain behaviors. "If it works, it *must* be right" is the pragmatic mantra along with "the end *justifies* the means." How many lives have to be destroyed and how many children must die before we stop lying to ourselves about the "musts" and the "justifies" of this pseudo-medical pragmatism?

If we then consider the treatment of ADHD to be experimental, we need to look at the accepted guidelines for such and ask some hard questions. To review, the ten points of the Nuremberg code are listed below with commentary specific to the issue of the use of medications in the treatment of ADHD in children.

1. The voluntary consent of the human subject is absolutely essential.

> This raises the issue of consent yet again. Adding the statement from the Declaration of Helsinki regarding a child needing to assent to the therapy raises serious questions as well. In addition, it is presumed subjects are given a thorough description of the therapy and in fact, they are not. Neither parents nor children are truly informed about the treatment being given. They are expected to *conform* to the institutions "request" and, though not explicitly stated, if they do not, serious consequences may result. Few are speaking the truth to the millions of children and parents caught up in the whirlwind of the ADHD mental health machine.

2. The experiment should be such as to yield fruitful results for the good of society, unprocurable by any other means of study, and not random and unnecessary in nature.

A key here is the phrase "unprocurable by *any* other means... unnecessary in nature." Many so-called ADHD children, whose parents have decided to take a non-pharmaceutical route, have seen their children flourish. A change to a more stimulating or challenging academic environment or a change in diet or more robust structure and discipline at home is certainly "procurable other means." Applying God's Word to sinful living is also another means (and a permanent one at that!). The use of drugs whose actions we do not understand and whose chemical structure is remarkably similar to cocaine seems entirely "unnecessary in nature" when suitable alternatives exist. Moreover, when discussing the good of society, what exactly determines good and who is society? Is good considered drugging children to a stupor so that the teacher and other students are not bothered...or so the teacher does not have to utilize creative teaching methods...or so the school does not have to hire additional teachers or paraprofessional teacher's aides...or so the parents do not have to deal with little Archie...or so the greater society avoids a potentially problematic individual later in life...and the list goes on...?

3. The experiment should be so designed and based on the results of animal experimentation and a knowledge of the natural history of the disease or other problem under study that the anticipated results will justify the performance of the experiment.

    Concerning ADHD, there are at least two problems under this particular point. First, behavior flows from thinking which flows from the spiritual heart. Because man is made in the image and likeness of God, he is different from the animals. Thus, animal experimentation with behavior cannot be generalized to humans. Animals do not possess the heart/mind/soul man has been given as a result of being made in God's likeness and image. The brain of a rat and the brain of a child are so vastly different that one would be hard pressed to draw meaningful conclusions when attempting to compare one to the other when discussing feeling, thinking and behaving. Second, this point refers to the *natural history of the disease* and ADHD is not a disease. There has never been any scientific data to support the classification of ADHD as a disease. A collection of behaviors are simply a collection of behaviors. Lastly, the point refers to anticipated results. In the case of ADHD, what are the anticipated results? Little improvement in academic performance, non-existent long term outcomes data, and unknown long-term drug safety are hallmarks of ADHD drug treatment. Given that, whose interests are being met? It does not seem as if the child benefits. Is "improved" classroom behavior *justification* enough to put a child's future or their life at risk? What would happen to these same children of they were raised in a structured home and school environment with interesting teachers and clear expectations and discipline? What if they received extra tutoring in math and reading, medical testing for real medical problems and a healthy diet? How would they respond if they were raised according to biblical standards?

4. The experiment should be so conducted as to avoid all unnecessary physical and mental suffering and injury.

Though the pharmaceutical and medical industries do not make it a point to discuss, there are frequent and severe side effects to all the amphetamine and amphetamine-like drugs used in the treatment of ADHD. As has been stated, these drugs have not been studied for a length of time exceeding fourteen weeks in robust clinical trials. We do not know what they will do to the body when given for lengthy periods of time. There *are* physical effects of the drugs. Some call this efficacy, but look at what is lost as we deem the drugs effective: creativity, spontaneity, joy and in many cases, childhood itself. Is this not mental suffering? Should we not consider all the children who have died or who have suffered unalterable brain or other organ damage as having been injured? Looking at the point above, we need to focus on the word "unnecessary." When is it ever necessary to risk harming a child with a drug when there are reasonable alternatives?

5. No experimentation should be conducted where there is an *a priori* reason to believe that death or disabling injury will occur; except, perhaps, in those experiments where the experimental physicians also serve as subjects.

    Though the *reported* serious side effects are rare in comparison to the total number of children and adults taking these medications, we must return to the issue of the unknown and the fact that this is indeed experimentation. The pharmaceutical industry is not about to fund research that may uncover irrefutable evidence of the harm these drugs cause. They will claim research of the long term nature needed to determine a true outcome is far too expensive to conduct. They only want to fund short-term studies where "efficacy" can be demonstrated but where serious side effects are almost impossible to detect. Once the drug is on the market and widely available, they know few physicians will take the time to report side effects, unless a death occurs. This is known as "underreporting" and it complicates safety assessments on all drugs in the United States. As such, we really have no idea (unknown) what the true incidence of side-effects and injury is in terms of physical damage. In addition, we may never know what was lost in terms of the "personhood" of those exposed to these drugs for long periods of time.

6. The degree of risk to be taken should never exceed that determined by the humanitarian importance of the problem to be solved by the experiment.

    This is a wonderful question when we consider who is actually receiving the benefit from ADHD drug treatment. Is it society at large, the teacher, other students, or the parents? Is there really any benefit for the child being treated? Has thirty years of treating children with the scourge of ADHD made an impact on our society? Have we avoided some catastrophic societal collapse thanks to amphetamines? Clearly, the answer is no. Our society is on the moral decline and it is evident all around us. Have teachers benefited by making little Archie more docile? Perhaps on the surface, the answer is yes. However, it has robbed them of the opportunity to be increasingly creative and expressive in their own teaching techniques. What is not considered is the fact that most teachers are forced to maintain classes with far too many students and far too few resources to meet little Archie's learning needs. Moreover, Archie is not being disciplined nor is he seeing appropriate behavior being modeled at home. Parents are abdicating their parenting responsibilities to the schools and the schools, in turn, are abdicating to the psychologists. The mental health professionals invariably turn to medications thanks to the theories of biological psychiatry and chemical imbalances. The problems began in the heart and they are not going to be rectified anywhere else. What about benefit to the child? Unfortunately, this too falls short. Children are anesthetized into a placid state of existence which robs them of one of life's most wonderful gifts, childhood itself.

7. Proper preparations should be made and adequate facilities provided to protect the experimental subject against even remote possibilities of injury, disability, or death.

How many parents are instructed in the true risks of amphetamine therapy? The overwhelming majority are told of a mild little yellow pill that will help Archie concentrate. The arguments listed above apply here as well. Parents and children are not informed. They are simply expected to conform…or else….

8. The experiment should be conducted only by scientifically qualified persons. The highest degree of skill and care should be required through all stages of the experiment of those who conduct or engage in the experiment.

When experiments are conducted, there are significant safeguards in place to protect the welfare of the research subjects. Based on the arguments contained in this book, it is evident amphetamine (and many other mental health) drug therapy(ies) in children is (are) nothing more than human experimentation. Sadly, the safety procedures required in formal research are not applied and children and families are being harmed.

School administrators, teachers, nurses, social workers and psychologists are simply not qualified scientifically to conduct these experiments and many physicians do not possess the specialized expertise necessary to safely administer these drugs to children. Parents are subjecting their children to sometimes decades-long experimentation without being fully informed. There is a time concern if little Archie is injured and needs emergency surgery. Perhaps not every question will be answered in depth. However, in treating ADHD, parents will often conform to the wishes of the so-called experts without taking the time to adequately explore all of the risks and options available to them. Unfortunately, the days of blindly trusting "ole' Doc Smith" are long gone.

9. During the course of the experiment the human subject should be at liberty to bring the experiment to an end if he has reached the physical or mental state where continuation of the experiment to him to be impossible.

This point again hearkens back to the argument given in number one above. When parents see what the drugs do to their children and wish to "opt out," they are again faced with the threat of State intervention. In addition, the risk of suicide is increased in those who are withdrawing from amphetamine and amphetamine-like drugs.

10. During the course of the experiment the scientist in charge must be prepared to terminate the experiment at any stage, if he has probable cause to believe, in the exercise of good faith, superior skill and careful judgment required of him that a continuation of the experiment is likely to result in injury, disability, or death to the experimental subject.[84] This point too has been discussed in detail above.

Why should we be so concerned about the growing use of drugs in the treatment of ADHD? Millions of children have been treated with powerful stimulant drugs similar to cocaine and methamphetamine. In a study in 2005, it was found that 10% of teens abuse Ritalin and

---

[84] *Ibid.*

Adderall.[85]   Since 1987 when ADHD was added to the DSM, there has been a 900% increase in the number of children diagnosed with ADHD and a 665% increase in the number of children being treated with amphetamine and amphetamine-like drugs.[86] This has led sales of these drugs in the United States to top $1.3 billion per year.   All of this is represented not by conclusive medical science or even sound theory.   It is supported by an industry whose greed is unprecedented. Thomas Szasz, noted professor, researcher, author said,

> "Since psychiatry is a pseudoscience, it is not surprising that psychiatrists are especially eager to be accepted as scientific experts.   Since they obviously cannot bring this about by discovering the causes and cures of mental diseases which - tragically for psychiatrists no less than for patients - do not exist, they have to do it by producing great quantities of gibberish. That is indeed the most constant and most frequent thing psychiatrists do, in speech as well as in print."[87]

As the psychiatrists have gone, so has the drug industry.   They are long on pseudo-scientific gibberish and short on science.   It is sadly analogous to asking an electrical engineer what time it is and having him explain to you in excruciating detail how a digital watch works. He takes great satisfaction in his knowledge and speech yet he has failed to answer the simple question. Psychiatrists and pharmaceutical scientists can expound for hours about their theories on this or that behavior or chemical, but neither can tell you what time it is.

Application

The key in new learning is application.   When a child is learning to walk, he applies this knowledge to exploring his world, thus leading to new learning and discovery for his benefit.   His life is never the same.   When the telephone lost its cord and then eventually became cellular, we applied this new learning for our benefit.   Our lives will

---

[85] Survey: 1 in 5 Teens Getting High on Medications, Over-Counter Drugs," News-item.com,2 June 2005

[86] Fred A.Baughman, Jr. "Transcript: Calls for Investigation into Diagnosis of ADHD," ABC Austria Online, March 23, 2000, Internet URL: http://www.abc.net.au; "The White House on Ritalin," New York Press, March 29 – April 4, 2000.

[87] Thomas S. Szasz, *The Therapeutic State: Psychiatry in the Mirror of Current Events*, (New York, NY.: Prometheus Books, 1984), p. 32.

never be the same. When scientists discovered the anti-bacterial properties of some molds, this new learning translated into numerous drugs to treat life-threatening infections and mankind benefited. Medicine has never been the same. As one arrives at this point in the book, the question that begs to be asked is, "Now what? How can I as a Christian parent, counselor, educator, or physician apply what is here?" Indeed, for some, this is new knowledge and it should be applied such that our lives are never quite the same.

For some, it may mean altering the counsel they give Christian parents on the subject of raising children. For others, it may alter the way children are raised, taught or disciplined. Still others may require a wholesale examination of the use of Scripture versus the use of "science." Parents may have to fight the public school system for what is right. Counselors may have to fight against the grain of "conventional wisdom" in counseling theory and application in order to do what is right by their counselees. Educators and physicians may have to seriously consider the validity of their thinking and practices in order to do what is right. Whatever the case, following God's prescription will never be popular. The world will push back. Recall John 16:33 where Jesus said, "I have said these things to you, that in me you may have peace. In the world you will have tribulation. But take heart; I have overcome the world." (ESV) Taking a stand for what is right when that stand contradicts the direction of the crowd is rarely easy or without difficulty. Jesus tells us we will have tribulation. We are responsible for being obedient because of two facts He states here. First, if we remain in Him, we will have peace. Second, He has already overcome the world and secured the victory. These promises do not say we will be trouble free. They do not say our lives will be carefree and easy. They say we will have problems, troubles, and challenges but that we can have peace because He has already secured the victory. Given that we are already victorious, it is time for us to take a stand. It is time for us to move from being *conformed* to being *informed*.

Based on the issues raised in this chapter, we must ask questions about the things we do not fully understand while resisting the urge to simply say the doctor or the psychologist knows best because of their training and experience. No one is more experienced in raising a given child than that child's parents. We must ask the hard questions and refuse to accept the standard replies that seem to satisfy so many. Some examples, based on the points of the Nuremburg Code would be:

1. Is ADHD or ADD a disease?
   a. How is it diagnosed?
   b. What objective medical tests are used to determine the presence or absence of the disease?
2. What is the human research-supported short and long-term benefits to using this medication?
   a. Define long-term.
   b. How long do you foresee my child being on this medication?
3. What are the
   a. true risks,
   b. side-effects,
   c. long-term effects,
   d. costs of this medication?
4. What serious or life-threatening adverse events have been observed with this medication both in clinical trials and in clinical practice?
   a. What problems have you encountered in your patients taking this medication?
   b. Have there been any deaths reported?
5. What irrefutable scientific data is available to support the use of the medication in children?
6. What are the alternatives to using medication?

   Other questions to ask of the schools and of yourself as a parent could be:
7. What alternatives are there in the classroom for my child?
   a. How many students are in my child's class?
   b. Are there any other children exhibiting similar behaviors?
   c. Is there a teacher's aide in the room?
   d. Is the classroom a stimulating environment for learning?
   e. Do I need to consider getting a tutor?
8. What can I (we) do in the home to assist Archie?
9. Should we seek counseling?

These represent only a starting point. Hard questions should be asked of teachers, principals, social workers, psychologists and anyone who is recommending treatment with medications. An evaluation of the home environment is also needed. Archie's behavior may not be directly related to his upbringing, but there may be changes that need to be implemented in order to assist him in changing. In short, we need to be much better informed about the decisions being made as parents. We need to look within our own homes as well as at school and elsewhere. It is imperative we become a more informed people able to understand what the world is suggesting and balancing that against how we are commanded in Scripture. Not to be melodramatic, but your child's life may be at stake.

The key for parents, counselors, physicians and others interested or involved with ADHD is to be fully and completely informed about the medical and behavioral aspects of children labeled as such. While there may be some organic medical issues related to allergies or diet, the predominant problem is most often spiritual in nature. That being the case, the prescription for change is not found in a drug, nor is it found in behavior modification. True change is a change in heart. The philosophies of man labeled as psychological theories are not sufficient to elicit true change. Admittedly, people's behavior may "improve" with psychological counseling and/or medications for some period of time. The improvement may even be long-standing. However, the underlying heart remains unchanged, carnal, worldly, guilty, rebellious and even hardened toward God and the things of God. In short, behavioral change is not enough and the pharmaceutical masking of behavior is even worse. It may satisfy the school officials when little Archie is subdued, but there is not real change. In fact, Archie simply goes from being disruptive and defiant to being "stoned" and defiant.

Alternatives

It is likely many of Archie's behaviors are sinful and in the absence of an organic, physical cause, we must consider a therapy not directed at a non-existent, man-created "disease", but a therapy directed at the sinful behaviors, thoughts and feelings emanating from Archie's spiritual heart. Archie must be *"sanctified in truth"* as in John 17:17. Now this is not some magical powder that can be sprinkled over Archie like a mystical scene from the *Lord of the Rings* or *Harry Potter*. Rather, it is an effort that will require work from not only Archie himself, but also his parents and perhaps a qualified biblical counselor. It will be a difficult process, but not an impossible one. God does not provide the command to change and leave us without the means. As change begins to take root in Archie's life, he will be encouraged as the Holy

Spirit works in him through the Scriptures. As the old man is put off and the new put on, the benefits will become evident to Archie: God is working in his life to make him more like Christ. God has a plan and a purpose for his life and He is not going to be satisfied leaving him in a persistently sinful state. Despite what those in the medical community and those in the ADHD lobbying groups (like C.H.A.D.D.) may espouse, sin is not cured with a little yellow pill. It is not cured through a cocktail of snake oil and eye of newt masquerading as the irrefutable scientific answer to Archie's fidgetiness. It is cured by the blood of the Sinless One who died so that we may have life and that we may have it more abundantly.

Archie is commanded to change. He is to put forth whatever effort is necessary in order to become more like Christ. But Archie's efforts are not without a guide. He is not walking the path alone. God has provided His Word and the Holy Counselor to direct Archie to Christ-likeness. God's prescription for change is to put off the old, sinful self, renew the spirit of the mind through Scripture, and to put on the new, righteous self in the likeness of Christ (Ephesians 4:17, 22-24). God does not intend for us to be a slave to sin (Romans 6:6) but to put it off so that it no longer masters us. This process of sanctification is intended and expected from all of God's children and little Archie is no exception.[88] As with all humans, Archie has become habituated to certain unrighteous behaviors and patterns of thinking and feeling. These are what must be put off and then replaced with their righteous counterparts. As in 2 Timothy 3:16-17, Archie must be taught, rebuked (thus bringing about conviction), corrected, and trained in righteousness. This last step is imperative to real change. Because real change is a spiritual event, it is not enough to simply stop doing "wrong" things. "Right" things must replace "wrong" things and the "right" things are those found in Scripture.

Encouragement

As biblical counselors, we have the privilege of seeing people changed regularly by the power of the Holy Spirit through Scripture. Those who change would tell you it was a difficult, sometimes frustrating experience. They would also tell you it was one of the best

---

[88] We are assuming throughout that Archie is a believer. If he is not, the counsel he should be receiving from his parents should be directed toward leading Archie to the saving knowledge of Jesus Christ.

experiences of their lives. To have victory over an area of life where sin reigned is one of those oft mentioned "mountain tops" of the Christian experience. To see a counselee go through this process of change is a blessing beyond words. We say this to offer encouragement to those dealing with ADHD individually or in their family. Real change, not the chameleon-like false change of psychology, is available for every child of God who desires to be more like Christ. For those who will honor God and God's Word for what it is (Truth with a capital T) and who will actually do what His Word tells us to do, you will find that God is 100% faithful and that His counsel is 100% effective. No drug, secular counseling method, counselor, or herbal "cure" can promise that kind of success. God's prescription has side effects, however. When individual problems are handled in this manner, families are restored; married couples who were on the brink of divorce are again like newlyweds; people who struggled and failed with anger, depression, anxiety, selfishness, pornography and a host of other problems enjoy the fruits of the Spirit and the blessings of being in fellowship with God. And let us not forget about little Archie. God's prescription is not only indicated for adults, but it is also indicated for children. In many instances, the "pill" does not seem to be as bitter with children as it is with adults, perhaps because of the length of time adults have had to nourish their unrighteous habits. What a gift indeed it is for a child to begin to learn how to effect real change in his life. In short, there is great hope for Archie. He too can change to become more like Jesus. Archie's change may require his parents to change too, but in God's Providence, perhaps this was part of His plan for the entire family. Remember what Jesus said about the children?

> **Then some children were brought to Him so that He might lay His hands on them and pray; and the disciples rebuked them. But Jesus said, "Let the children alone, and do not hinder them from coming to Me; for the kingdom of heaven belongs to such as these." After laying His hands on them, He departed from there** (Matthew 19:13-15).

God is indeed faithful and it is His desire that we all change. As Archie and his parents change, they will be a blessing and an encouragement to others. God will be honored, praised and glorified. Hearts will be changed and He will be lifted up. Thank God for every Archie, for in him is the opportunity to see God work in a wonderful and miraculous way.

Chapter 11

The Process of Biblical Change: Putting Off and Putting On

All Scripture is inspired by God and profitable for teaching, for reproof, for correction, for training in righteousness; that the man of God may be adequate, equipped for every good work.

Apostle Paul
2 Timothy 3:16-17

Little Archie, like all children and adults, will habituate himself to speak, behave, think and be motivated in ways that are displeasing to God. Left on his own Archie will be filled with his own ways (Proverbs. 1:30, 31; 14:14). He will cause a great deal of pain, heartache and embarrassment to his parents. "A child left to himself disgraces his mother" (Proverbs 29:15, NIV). Archie's parents must train him, with the help of the Holy Spirit and the Scriptures, to speak, behave, think and be motivated biblically (Deuteronomy 6:7-9 and Ephesians 6:4). They must teach Archie that God has also given him a goal of pleasing God (2 Corinthians 5:9).

Step One: Teaching

Accurate doctrine is very important. Biblical counseling is not simply counseling using Bible verses, reducing a person's problems to theological slogans, or meaningless clichés and applying them to the most recent psychological theories. Parents who counsel using the Bible must be conversant on essential doctrines such as sin, regeneration, justification, sanctification, repentance, and forgiveness. They are knowledgeable of how man's nature prior to and after the Fall impacts counseling and change. They understand that every truth in

Scripture has implications for living. They know no doctrine is given for merely abstract reasons; therefore, parents must become familiar with the entire body of Christian doctrine. They will probe into the Scriptures, coming to correct interpretations of passages, thinking through the implications of doctrine. They will be continually growing in their understanding and application of how doctrine relates to life. They will, with the help of the Holy Spirit, become a workman in the Word who will not be "ashamed" because they have consistently been "accurately handling the word of truth" (2 Timothy 2:15). The Bible is the standard and is crucial to counseling, and Archie's parents cannot neglect any part. Paul urged Timothy to "Retain the standard of sound words which you have heard from me, in the faith and love which are in Christ Jesus" (2 Timothy 1:13). It was vital that Timothy hold fast to what Paul had taught him. Archie's parents must teach Archie doctrine if they are going to help him put off sin and put on righteousness.

The counsel parents give must be totally biblical in content. The content will consist of any command or combination of commands referred to by Jesus in Matthew 28:20. Jesus said, the true method of discipleship or counseling is "teaching them to *observe* what Christ commanded" (italics ours). The emphasis of Christ's words is not on facts to be learned but rather truth to be lived. It is knowledge for the sake of implementation, not just the sake of knowledge. The objective of discipleship or counseling is that Archie will be conformed to the image of Christ.

Every other counseling system's goal is to lead their counselees to change, however, none of them can agree on what kind of change. They are out to change people, but into what? It goes back to the question of standards. Parents that counsel biblically are not committed to men's standards, but God's. They accept God's standards which are unaffected by sin. Therefore, they can know for certain what Archie should look like at the end of counseling. Jesus said, "A pupil is not above his teacher; but everyone, after he has been fully trained, will be like his teacher" (Luke 6:40). The word "trained" refers to the successful effort of retraining Archie to put-off sinful habits and put-on the righteous alternative habits of behavior. Again, Archie should look like Jesus Christ.

Parents who have experienced the difficulty of having an inattentive, hyperactive and/or impulsive child need hope. They must learn that hope comes from the Bible. Hope produces joy in difficult times (Proverbs 10:28; Romans 5:2-3; 12:12; 1 Thessalonians 4:13), perseverance (Romans 8:24-25), confidence (2 Corinthians 3:12; Philippians 1:20), steadfastness (1 Thessalonians 1:3), zeal (Romans 12:11; 1 Timothy 4:10), and stability (Hebrews 6:19). Hope is essential to the process of change. Adults or children who have been stigmatized with psychological labels, and have been told they are sick or not normal, need hope. Giving biblical hope is a skill which every parent needs to master. They must give hope along the way as they sort through the maze of Archie's problems and the consequences. They know how, and teach Archie, to relate biblical doctrines and principles to specific problems. They understand that the ultimate goal is not just to help Archie through the immediate problems, but to help him develop the biblical skills and knowledge to avoid and handle future problems God's way.

This instruction will give Archie hope to move ahead in the counseling process. Hope is essential to persevering and solving problems. Paul wrote, "For whatever was written in earlier times was written for our instruction, that through *perseverance* and the encouragement of Scriptures we might have *hope*" (Romans 15:4, italics ours). Hope leads to perseverance. A runner will persevere if he has hope of winning the race. Holy Scriptures, not psychology, are used to offer encouragement and hope to Archie. Paul continued, "Now may the God of hope fill you with all joy and peace believing, that you may abound in hope by the power of the Holy Spirit" (Romans 15:13). All the efforts of Archie's parents will be unproductive unless they instill biblical hope in him.[89]

Parents must be knowledgeable in order to teach their child the Biblical doctrine and dynamics of habit. Often parents do not understand how the change process works. Many Christian parents fail to help their children change because they concentrate only on breaking a sinful habit. It is all about will-power and prayer. We never minimize the importance of prayer however, there is more to do than pray. The Bible does not teach us to *break* sinful habits, but to *replace* them with godly habits.

When God created mankind he made him with the capacity to formulate habits. Without this ability a person would have to think about *everything* he does or says. Every action would have to be thought

---

[89] See Jay Adam's book *The Christian Counselor's Manual* for a more in-depth discussion on how to give hope to your counselee.

out and performed in a methodical, meticulous, and laborious way. The blessing of habit allows a person to carry out complicated tasks comfortably and automatically. It makes writing a letter to a friend possible without relearning how to write the letters of the alphabet. Walking, talking and literally, thousands of different things and combinations of things are made possible by man's ability to create habits. The ability to develop habits is truly a blessing. However, indwelling sin makes it easy to develop sinful habits. Training children to develop godly habits is what Christ-likeness is all about.[90]

Over time, and by practice, people become habituated to certain tasks. The writer of Hebrews wrote about habits when he said, "But solid food is for the mature, who because of *practice* have their senses *trained* to discern good and evil" (Hebrews 5:14, italics ours). People become habituated to many behaviors and attitudes. For example, greed is a learned behavior or habit. Peter wrote: "Having eyes full of adultery and that never cease from sin, enticing unstable souls, having a heart *trained* in greed, accursed children" (2 Peter 2:14, italics ours). Some people are never satisfied or content. Paul was one of those people, but he said he learned how to be content. He wrote, "Not that I speak from want; for I have *learned* to be content in whatever circumstances I am" (Philippians 4:11, italics ours). People who have sinful habits can change. Jeremiah wrote: "You also can do good who are *accustomed* to doing evil" (Jeremiah 13:23, italics ours). Paul wrote to Titus concerning believers who had been enslaved or habituated to sinful practices, but had changed. He said, "For we also once *were* foolish ourselves, disobedient, deceived, *enslaved* to various lusts and pleasures, spending our life in malice and envy, hateful, hating one another" (Titus 3:3, italics ours). When Paul wrote to the Corinthian believers, he reminded some of them about their past sinful practices which they had successfully put off. He wrote:

> **Or do you not know that the unrighteous shall not inherit the kingdom of God? Do not be deceived; neither fornicators, nor idolaters, nor adulterers, nor effeminate, nor homosexuals, nor thieves, nor {the} covetous, nor drunkards, nor revilers, nor swindlers,**

---

[90] When we speak of developing godly habits we are not referring to a form of behavior modification. We are referring to the process of sanctification which is produced by the Holy Spirit using God's Word. The change of habits we refer to are not superficial external behaviors, but a change of heart that leads to a change of one's motives, thoughts, behavior and feelings.

> **shall inherit the kingdom of God.** *And such were some of you*; **but you were washed, but you were sanctified, but you were justified in the name of the Lord Jesus Christ, and in the Spirit of our God** (1 Corinthians 6:9-11, italics ours).

While habit, a blessing from God, makes life easier and more comfortable, habit can also be a curse. Sinful habits are the source of Archie's problems. Archie has become habituated to sinful behaviors and attitudes. Sanctification involves helping him put off sinful habits and put on the biblical alternative habits. It is putting off the deeds of the flesh and putting on the fruit of the Spirit (Galatians 5). Habits are learned ways of living, and therefore can be unlearned and replaced. Habits are formed when something is done repeatedly. Over time thinking or behavior becomes habitual.

The tendency of people in our psycholgized culture is to talk about the out-of-control feeling of certain "behaviors." They reason about the "external" things (environment, etc.) or internal things ("disease, chemical imbalance," etc.) controlling them. In contrast, the Bible brings in the crucial element of the heart. The heart controls man. Man is responsible. The sinful behaviors and attitudes are desired and pursued by men. The allure to sin is rooted in the heart, and as it is practiced over a period of time, becomes a habit. That is the fundamental nature of sin. All people sin, all people sin differently, all people sin habitually. What psychology calls addictive, compulsive, or sick (said to have a biological or genetic cause although never substantiated) behavior (the disease model), the Bible calls habitual sinful behavior. In the sin model the heart is the center of behavior. The heart, which is biased against God and for self, is the source of the problem. It is not an outside force that has invaded one's body, or chemicals gone haywire; it is one's own desire. The problem is not God or the circumstances; it is the individual himself. Sin, not biology or genetics, is Archie's principle problem.

Sanctification, as mentioned earlier, is the work of God in the believer and the believer's work. The forces at work in the sanctification process are the Holy Spirit, God's Word, and the regenerate believer. It is a human as well as a divine activity. The Spirit of God incites the believer to work. Man is not passive. Paul said, "For it is God who is at work in you, both to will and to work for His good pleasure" (Philippians 2:13). Paul said that he "labors," but at the same time it is

God's "power which mightily works within me" (Colossians 1:29). It is not an easy process. Present in the believer is the old self. Strenuous effort must be exerted to put off the old self and its sinful habits and put on the new self. Change is hard, but not impossible. Persistent effort, discipline and self-control must be exercised if spiritual progress is to be made. The believer's union with Christ makes possible the reality that the "body of sin [i.e., sinful habits that are in the body] might be done away with, that we should no longer be slaves to sin" (Romans 6:6, brackets ours).

The Christian's relationship to God's Law as it pertains to sanctification is the theme of Romans seven. Paul writes, "For while we were in the flesh, the sinful passions, which were aroused by the Law, were at work in the members of our body to bear fruit for death" (Romans 7:5). In the previous chapters the apostle built his case for justification by faith apart from the Law. The Law exposes sin, but cannot remove sin. Paul continued, "I would not have come to know sin except through the Law; for I would not have known about coveting if the Law had not said, 'You shall not covet'" (Romans 7:7).

The Apostle Paul, up to this point, had been talking about a believer's past. He explained how Christians have died to sin (Romans 6:2), been buried with Christ through baptism, and raised from the dead (6:4). But then Paul changes the tense in the next chapter. He wrote, "For we know that the Law is spiritual; but I am of flesh, sold into bondage to sin (Romans 7:14, italics ours). He wrote *I am* and not *I was* of flesh. He continued to write in the present tense. "For that which I am doing" (Romans 7:15), "For I know" (7:18), and "but I see" (7:23).

Paul emphasized there is nothing wrong with the Law itself. The Law is spiritual, and good. Paul turns his eyes inward and bemoans the terrible fact that he himself was the problem. "I am," Paul said, "of the flesh and sold into bondage." He made similar statements earlier, of which this is a reference about yielding himself to be a slave to sin or righteousness (Romans 6:16-20). Sin is still in the body or members of the believer (6:12). There is a continuous fight to wage. It is for that reason Paul exhorts the believer to consider self dead, not let sin reign, and not go on presenting the members of his body to sin. Sanctification is hindered because Paul's body is habituated to sin. In spite of the fact he died to sin (status and position), he nevertheless was led and drawn by the habituated desires of the flesh. It was almost like he was still under the dominion and reign of sin. He wrote,

> **For that which I am doing, I do not understand; for I am not practicing what I would like to do, but I am doing the very thing I hate. But if I do the very thing I do not wish to do, I agree with the Law, confessing that it is good** (Romans 7:15-16).

The Christian, instead of being a slave to the sinful habits of the body, should "buffet" his body and make it a slave to him (1 Corinthians 9:27). The difficulty is, under the Law, he is not able to do what he desires to do. He does the opposite. The believer is still bound by sinful habits of the flesh (thinking and behavior), even though he is not in the flesh (status).

The Christian will always fail in his efforts toward Christ-likeness if he tries in his own strength to fight against his body. The Law cannot sanctify a person (Romans 8:3). Will-power is no match for the sinfully habituated flesh (Romans 7:15). The desire, will, and longing of the regenerate heart is to do right, but the "doing" is the problem (7:18). Another principle is hard at work in the members of his body waging a war against the law of his mind (7:23). The law is the habituation of the body to sin. This law permeates the members of the body and holds the believer captive. The captivity Paul talks about is the captivity of sinful habits. Habits are hard to put-off. They are like the anaconda that coils itself around you. As you wrestle to pull off one coil and free yourself, the serpent has coiled itself again. The body must be re-habituated. Sinful habits, such as those behaviors labeled ADHD, and other psychiatric "diseases," that have complicated life and relationships must be put off and the biblical alternative habits of living put on. Sanctification, the putting off of sinfulness and putting on of righteousness, is possible only through the Holy Spirit and Scripture.

Step Two: Rebuking and Conviction

The second step toward helping Archie change is rebuke. Rebuke brings conviction and flows out of teaching. In order to produce conviction, Archie's parents may have to teach new material or remind him what he was previously taught, but has not yet converted from theory into practice. His parents may need to further clarify biblical truth and how it applies to the particulars of Archie's situation.

Bringing Archie to conviction of sin is an important aspect toward permanent change. He must acknowledge that he has failed to live up to the standards of God's Word. Archie must understand he has sinned. In order to honor God he must confess, repent, and seek forgiveness. The goal of biblical counseling is to please God, not to benefit mom, dad, teachers and society. Any counseling that claims to be Biblical, but does not have pleasing God as its goal, is not biblical at all.

Many Christians do not believe that rebuke, which brings a counselee to conviction of sin, should be part of counseling. This attitude is consistent with a humanistic approach to counseling, but not with the biblical approach. Psychologist Carl Rogers' method of counseling is the preferred method taught in most Christian seminaries, and therefore is practiced by many pastors and laymen. Rogerian counseling is non-directive and non-confrontational. It is amazing to listen to evangelical pastors talk about counseling people and not rebuking them or directing them in what they need to do. One pastor said, "I don't think you should tell a person what to do. I think you should just listen and help them arrive at answers on their own." That attitude is typical of Rogerian counseling.

Much of what is called "Christian" counseling today is not aimed at bringing the counselee to conviction of sin. The aim is to make the counselee feel better about himself and/or realize his behavior is caused by a disorder of the brain. You do not rebuke a person because they have a "disease." It neglects the basic reason why a believer must change to please God. Honoring God and His Word, not boosting self-esteem, calling sin sickness, is the goal of all counseling that purports to be biblical. Archie needs to be confronted with his sinful behavior. Archie's parents need to help him understand that his behavior causes him not only to be in an unreconciled state with his school teacher, but he is in an unreconciled state with God. Any attempt to change Archie without first seeking to restore his relationship with God will only result in an outward, pharisaical change.

Archie needs to be rebuked and brought under conviction for his self-centeredness, not paying attention, interrupting others, and getting out of his seat (these are not symptoms of disease). Rebuke and conviction is a prerequisite to repentance. Jesus reminds us of this when he said, "Those whom I love, I reprove and discipline; therefore be zealous and repent" (Revelations 3:19). Conviction that leads to repentance is part of the disciplinary and change process. While it is possible for a person to be convicted of sin and not repent;

it is not possible for a person to sincerely repent without first being convicted.

Parents should keep in mind that praise and commendation should be carefully inserted in these situations to assure the child of your love for him or her. Convicting little sinners like Archie is a regular and continuous parental activity. Sincere praise, not falsely praising children's virtues should be a constant practice. When reproof is given against a background of praise and approval, it helps to insure the child will develop a balanced view of their strengths and weakness, virtues and sinful habits.

Step Three: Correction

To rebuke Archie is to bring a biblical case against him for his sin. It is like a prosecuting attorney who presents evidence against the accused. He tears down the accused person's defenses (calling sin sickness) in order to prove his guilt. Rebuke knocks Archie to the ground, but correction stands him back up again. God's Word not only exposes what is wrong, but fixes what has gone wrong—correction.

The process of correcting Archie's behavior and attitudes is explained in Ephesians 4 when Paul wrote, "that, in reference to your former manner of life [habits], you lay aside the old self, which is being corrupted in accordance with the lusts of deceit" (v. 22, brackets mine). Correction means laying aside a sinful practice. However, laying aside a sinful practice must begin by repenting, confessing, and seeking the forgiveness of the person or persons Archie has offended. Correction must always include confession of sin and the seeking of forgiveness. Archie needs to confess his sin and guilt and ask forgiveness of those he had behaved disrespectfully and disobediently toward.

Step Four: Training in Righteousness

The Bible looks at behavior in ethical terms. The Scriptures refer to behavior in terms of righteousness or unrighteousness whereas psychiatry refers to behavior as healthy or unhealthy. When Archie refuses to do his school assignments, wait his turn, or disobeys the teacher, his behavior is unrighteousness. If his parents refer to his sin as sickness then Archie is a victim and a patient and is no longer responsible for his actions.

Correcting Archie's behavior is not enough. Lasting outward change requires inward change. New habits of living must be developed. Laying aside "Often has difficulty sustaining attention in tasks or play activities," is only the first step in the two step process of putting off sin and putting on righteousness. Archie needs to put off the habit of not paying attention by putting on the habit of paying attention. Paul said, 'and put on the new self, which in the likeness of God has been created in righteousness and holiness of truth" (Ephesians 4:24). In order to make himself more like Christ, Archie needs to renew or change his thinking (Ephesians 4:23). He needs to think biblically. He does not have a disease, he has bad habits. He needs to set his mind on things above (Colossians 3:2). He needs to prepare his mind for action (1 Peter 1:13). It is not enough just to put off the old ways. Archie cannot put off a sinful habit and then neglect or postpone developing a new alternative habit. The old sinful habit or something worse will return filling the vacuum. Therefore, if Archie's parents have not helped him *learn* to pay attention, his mind will wander and he will not pay attention.

A person's failure to change when he wants to change can be very discouraging. Failure to bring about change that is permanent is the sad testimony of many Christians who are living (habituated) in a sin. They have been taught doctrine (teach). They have been convicted of sin (rebuke). They know what they need to stop doing and know what they need to do (correction). The problem is they change their ways for a time, but then they fall back into the old habit or way of living. Their sanctification is stalled. They never move to step four; putting on godly habits of living.

The fourth step is essential to change. As we mentioned earlier, to resist change is to grieve the Holy Spirit. Change that sticks is vitally important to the process of sanctification. Sanctification is more than just learning what the Bible teaches about a specific behavior or attitude. Sanctification involves radical and drastic change. Unfortunately, many Christians think directive counseling that insists on radical change must be left to the mental health specialist. What many believers do not realize is that psychiatry's beliefs and methods are antithetical to the Scriptures. Though habits are hard to change, they are not impossible to change. Habits are learned and can be unlearned. Personality is not set in stone, but is fluid. Personality can be changed. God changed Jacob into Israel. God changed impetuous and impulsive Peter into the great preacher of Pentecost. God changed the prideful Saul of Tarsus into Paul, who called himself the chief of all sinners. Archie can change too!

True biblical sanctification involves much more than changing a person's behavior. Biblical change is concerned with changing Archie. It is a spiritual process that involves four persons: the Holy Spirit, Archie, and his mother and father who come alongside him to minister the Word. Archie's parents use the difficulties he is experiencing at home and school to bring him closer to God (Romans 8:28). Being "conformed to the image of His Son" is the single most important characteristic of those who change, and therefore must be the number one factor in the mind of his parents.

The change of a behavior or activity is not the sort of change Archie's parents are striving for. This kind of change occurs under certain conditions and is temporary. They are not so much interested in behavior modification, but in real, substantial heart change. The goal is not merely that Archie pay attention to his school teacher when he or she is speaking, but that Archie himself changes to please God. Archie is not always inattentive, just as a drunkard is not always drunk. Just because Archie is not manifesting those behaviors consistent with the label of ADHD *now* or the drunkard is not drunk *now* does not mean there has been change. A pause or break in the sinful activity is not a sign of permanent change. The person *himself* must change. Jesus said, "For out of the heart come evil thoughts, murders, adulteries, fornications, thefts, false witness, slanders" (Matthew 15:19). Real change means Archie must be different at the heart level.

Paul wrote, "This I say therefore, and affirm together with the Lord, that you *walk no longer* just as the Gentiles also walk, in the futility of their mind" (Ephesians 4:17, italics ours). "Walk no longer" is a command to change. Paul was not calling upon believers to give up doing some unacceptable act or deed. Paul was calling on them to change their "manner of life" (4:22). The phrase, "put on the new self" implied the radical characteristics of the change God required (4:24). It was like becoming a new man with a new mind (4:23). Archie must change from being a child who does not pay attention, gets out of his seat, interrupts others, and does not wait his turn, into a child with self-control, patience and humility. Jay Adams said:

> *Change is a two-factored process.* These two factors always must be present in order to effect genuine change. Putting off will not be permanent without putting on.

Putting on is hypocritical as well as temporary, unless it is accompanied by putting off.[91]

There are many examples of this two-factored process of change. For example, Paul wrote, "laying aside falsehood [put off]," and "speak truth, each on of you, with his neighbor, for we are members of one another [put on]" (Ephesians 4:25, brackets ours). "Let him who steals steal no longer [put off]; but rather let him labor, performing with his own hands what is good, in order that he may have something to share with him who has need [put on]" (Ephesians 4:28, brackets ours). "Let no unwholesome word proceed out of your mouth [put off], but only such a word as is good for edification according to the need of the moment, that it may give grace to those who hear [put on]" Ephesians 4:29, brackets ours). There are put off and put on verses for every conceivable behavior and attitude.[92]

Paul wrote to Timothy, "But have nothing to do with worldly fables fit only for old women. On the other hand, *discipline yourself for the purpose of godliness*" (1 Timothy 4:7, italics ours). A person does not become godly by sitting in a pew and absorbing godliness from his environment. A person becomes godly by *practicing* godliness. Archie's parents must teach him to put off his inattentiveness by putting on attentiveness. This is done by practice. Archie was not born with the behavior labeled ADHD, but was habituated to it by years of practice.

Correction or making adjustments in Archie's behavior is not enough. Unless there is permanent change, he will fall back into his old way or habit. Putting off (correction) will not be permanent without putting on the biblical alternative habit. Archie's parents must not allow him to complain that he has tried unsuccessfully to quit some sin. Will-power and determination is no match for a child enslaved to a sin. In cases like Archie's where a particular sin reigns, deciding not to sin anymore is useless without step four. Archie must replace the sinful habit with the righteous habit that pleases God. Only then will he "change."

---

[91] Jay Adams, *The Christian Counselor's Manual*. (Grand Rapids, MI: Zondervan Publishing House, 1973), p. 177, italics in the original.

[92] See also Romans 12:14-21; 13:12-14; 1 Corinthians 6:18-20; 7:5; 15:33-34; 2 Corinthians 10:5; Galatians 5:19-23; 6:3-4; Ephesians 5:15-17; 6:4; Philippians 2:3-4; 3:13; Hebrews 10:23-25; 1 Peter 1:13-15; 2:11-12; 3:9. This is just a sample list. There are thousands of put off put on verses. See also *Transformed Into His Likeness: A Handbook for Putting Off Sin and Putting On Righteousness* by Armand P. Tiffe published by Focus Publishing, Bemidji, Minnesota.

Chapter 12
Conclusion: Is the
Bible Really Enough?[93]

I suggest to you that nothing is more important in our present situation than just this one particular point. Philosophy has always been the cause of the church going astray, for philosophy means, ultimately, a trusting to human reason and human understanding.

D.M. Lloyd-Jones
Knowing the Times

When psychology encroaches upon biblical territory by claiming jurisdictional authority in the counseling arena of what man "ought" to do, it is usurping God's domain. Psychology's illegitimate efforts cannot come to absolute conclusions about life, since at its heart psychology is only one fallible man telling another fallible man what to do. Arrogance abounds in such an environment. Only the divinely inspired Word of God has authority to do that.

John Street
Think Biblically

Man's mind is the greatest of all God's gifts. The ability man has of thinking in the abstract and contemplating himself distinguishes him above all the creatures God made. However, his greatest asset, because of his fallen condition, is his greatest danger. Satan is always particularly active in attacking the minds of men, the intellect and the understanding. The Apostle Paul wrote, "But I fear lest by any means,

---

[93] A Portion of this chapter has been adapted from the first chapter of the book *Self-Esteem: Are We Really Better Than We Think?* by David M. Tyler, Published by Personal Freedom Outreach (P.O. Box 26062, Saint Louis, Missouri 63136. www.pfo.org.).

as the serpent beguiled Eve through his subtlety, so your *minds* should be corrupted from the *simplicity* that is in Christ" (2 Corinthians 11:3, italics mine). At all times the devil is focused on turning the "simplicity" which is in Christ into something involved, complex and difficult. Hence the Apostle's warnings to be on guard against the adversary's attacks, which come along the route of the mind. Paul cautions believers, "Finally, be strong in the Lord and in the strength of his might. Put on the full armor of God, so that you will be able to stand firm against the schemes of the devil" (Ephesians 6:10-11). "See to it that no one takes you captive through philosophy (learning) and empty deception, according to the tradition of men, according to the elementary principles of the world, rather than according to Christ" (Colossians 2:8, KJV, parenthesis mine). "O Timothy, keep that which is committed to thy trust, avoiding profane and vain babblings, and oppositions of *science* (learning) falsely so called" (1 Timothy 6:20, KJV, parenthesis and italics ours).

The emphasis on the devil's assaults on man's mind had arisen in the early church and is perhaps at its greatest at the present. There is little doubt the greatest single enemy of the Christian faith is, and always has been, philosophy. Philosophy implies a final confidence in human reason, the power of man's mind and man's ability to arrive at truth. Authority is always the supreme and fundamental issue. The great watershed is do we accept the Bible as the Word of God, as the sole authority in all matters of faith and practice, including behavior, or do we not? Is the whole of my thinking concerning the nature of man governed by Scripture, or do I come with my particular model of psychology, putting Freud, Rogers or others forward as the ultimate standard and authority? These are urgent and important questions that everyone must answer. However, it is precisely at this point that the schemes or wiles of the devil prove so deceptive. Christians face the danger of being governed by what is called modern knowledge, and especially today, "science."

God's Word always begins with the presupposition that man, because he is fallen, sinful and finite, can never arrive at complete knowledge. The world through its wisdom did not come to know that God is a fact of the gospel message. The Bible starts with man's helplessness and his inability to arrive at truth. Truth is known only because God in His infinite mercy has been pleased to reveal it to us. Again Paul writes, "If any man among you thinks that he is wise in this age, he must become foolish, so that he may become wise" (1

Corinthians 3:18). In essence, Paul is saying to be wise you must stop being a philosopher. The philosopher is the man who is "wise in this age." Paul says he must become a fool. To become foolish means to admit your mind is insufficient and modern theories are useless in arriving at truth. It means you are absolutely dependent upon God's revelation. It means to confess that human reason, and the plethora of theories that come from reason, are vain. It is to realize the supreme achievement of reason is to show that there is a limit to reason. The main trouble today is man does not think there is a limit to reason and therefore, he continues to theorize and attempts to understand.

Increasingly, Christians are not hesitating to accept as reliable certain extra-biblical statements and authorities. The question of the relationship between the Bible and science is not as complex as the devil has made it out to be. As long as science deals with facts it should be accepted. Psychiatry and psychology are theories in the same way evolution is a theory. When men talk about evolution they are not being scientific, they are speaking as philosophers. When men talk about psychiatry and psychology they are not being scientific, they too, are speaking as philosophers. It is pure speculation. We must never accept speculation or supposition as authoritative. When considering the nature of man—why people do what they do and how to help them change—I must get my knowledge from the Bible. All other beliefs about the nature of man, put forward in the hundreds of psychological models, are competitive with God's Holy Word. We must never let the devil trick us into changing our authority because "science teaches…" We should not, nor do we need to go outside the realm of revelation. The Bible begins by telling man he cannot know truth, and has failed over and over in his attempt, and that he is blinded by the god of this world.

There can be no doubt that most of the troubles in the Church and the world today are due to a departure from the authority of the Bible. Man's philosophies have taken the place of God's revelation. Man's opinions are exalted. Secular leaders and Church leaders talk about "the advance of knowledge in psychiatry and its younger brother psychology," and "the assured results of such knowledge." The Bible becomes a book just like any other book, out of date in certain respects, wrong in other respects. The point is it is no longer a book on which you can rely implicitly when it comes to understanding people and their problems.

Sanctify Them In Truth!

Jesus said, "Sanctify them in truth; Thy word is truth" (John 17:17). The application of the word "sanctify," is related to Christians. It is God's work within believers purging, and cleansing them of sin. Unlike justification, which is immediate and once and for all, sanctification is progressive. The Apostle John describes God's method of sanctification through the medium of truth: His Word, which is truth. It is by bringing the believer into the knowledge of truth, and the believer implementing the truth or doctrine, that God works to produce sanctification. Sanctification is a primary object of God in the believer's salvation. Sanctification is set in motion at the moment of justification and is a life-long process.

Sanctification is the work of God within a Christian; however, it does not imply the believer does nothing. It is something the believer must put into practice. Paul writes, "Do not let sin reign in your mortal body so that you obey its lusts" (Romans 6:12). Sanctification is not a gift one receives. Sanctification is not a sudden experience of deliverance once and forever. Sin is going to remain in the body as long as it is mortal. Paul says, "Therefore, my beloved, as you have always obeyed, not as in my presence only, but now much more in my absence, work out your own salvation with fear and trembling; for it is *God who works* in you both to will and to do for His good pleasure" (Philippians 2:12-13, NKJV, italics ours). It is a perfect balance. God works in the believer in order that the believer may work. The paradoxical aspect of the command should not trouble the believer.

God works and man works. Paul always acknowledged both sides when he spoke of sanctification. Paul wrote in Galatians, "And we proclaim Him, admonishing every man and teaching every man with all wisdom, that we may present every man complete in Christ. And for this purpose also *I labor, striving* according to *His Power, which mightily works within me*" (Colossians 1:28-29, italics ours). Paul talks about his tireless labor against all difficulties, but clearly indicates his work is in concert with God's working within him. The work of Christ in us and for us does not exempt us from work, but rather excites it. That is why the Christian life is always described as a thing of energy. Sometimes we read of it as a pilgrimage, a race, or a wrestling match.

The process of sanctification is not a simple or easy process. One never reads in Scripture of the life of a Christian described as a flowery bed of ease. Sanctification must never be thought of as something that happens without a struggle or fight. The remnants of the old self are still present in the believer. The old self must be put off and the new self must be put on, and that involves unyielding and strenuous exertion. Paul writes, "Mortify therefore your members which are upon the earth" (Colossians 3:5, KJV), "flee immorality" (1 Corinthians 6:18) and "lay aside the deeds of darkness" (Romans 13:12). Jesus said a man must "deny himself" (Matthew 16:24). Paul exhorted Timothy, "discipline yourself for the purpose of godliness" (1 Timothy 4:7). A man who is habituated to a particular sin is not instructed to "let go and let God." He is not encouraged to take it passively to Christ and ask for deliverance. In fact, the Apostle Paul writes, "Let him who steals steal no longer; but rather he must labor, performing with his own hands" (Ephesians 4:28). The Christian must change. Paul said he buffets his body and makes it a slave (1 Corinthians 9:27). Change is hard, but not impossible. It involves exercising self-control and consistent effort. Nevertheless, the ultimate cause of all spiritual progress is God.

God's continuous work in the life of the believer causes him to be discontented with his sinful nature and inclinations. Paul experienced a great deal of discontent with the sin that dwelled in him when he referred to himself as a "wretched man" (Romans 7:24). On the other hand, God gives the believer holy desires, and aspirations. He longs to put off sin and put on righteousness. He never becomes satisfied, or justifies himself, but always seeks to deal with his sin. The paradox is that the more the believer puts off sin, the more he realizes there are other sinful behaviors and attitudes that need putting off (Romans 7:21-24).

Biological Psychiatry / Psychological Sanctification

In evangelicalism today, the Bible is not enough for sanctification. Yes, the Word of God is "a lamp to my feet, and a light to my path" (Psalm 119:105), but from a practical standpoint, what does that mean? After all, they say, we do not live in the same world in which the psalmist lived and wrote. The complexities of our day are too deep for biblical wisdom. The truth of the matter is all counseling issues are spiritual matters. Counseling is concerned with changing people's lives, their values, beliefs, relationships, attitudes, and behaviors. That is what the Bible is about. Paul writes, "Or do you not know that the unrighteous shall not inherit the kingdom of God?

Do not be deceived; neither fornicators, nor idolaters, nor adulterers, nor effeminate, nor homosexuals, nor thieves, nor the covetous, nor drunkards, nor revilers, nor swindlers, shall inherit the kingdom of God" (1 Corinthians 6:9-10). These are all issues common in counseling. Paul says to the Galatian believers, "Now the deeds of the flesh are evident, which are: immorality, impurity, sensuality, idolatry, sorcery, enmities, strife, jealousy, outbursts of anger, disputes, dissensions, factions, envying, drunkenness, carousing, and things like these, of which I forewarn you just as I forewarned you that those who practice such things shall not inherit the kingdom of God" (Galatians 5:19-21). These are the same problems that break up marriages, set children against their parents, and cause depression and anxiety. All counseling issues are Biblical issues.

Those who attempt to integrate Christian theology with psychology are convinced there is a need for a higher wisdom than Scripture offers. There is a need for someone with better resources than the Bible, prayer, and the Holy Spirit. Bona fide "professional" counselors, who understand how human nature functions, are needed. The kinds of counselors that are required are those, for example, trained in psychotherapy. People who are skilled psychotherapists claim they can look beneath the surface of people's behavior and reveal an unconscious network of defenses and painful feelings that are responsible for all sorts of emotional problems. Such counselors also allege to help Christians who are anxious, fearful, confused, or depressed, by filling in the gaps left in the Bible concerning the "child within." Counselors maintain they can help Christians experience the love and acceptance of Jesus Christ through self-discovery and self-esteem.

The "discovered" truths practiced by "Christian" psychologists have taken on the distinction once reserved for the Bible. So dedicated are they to their cherished misconceptions that they fail to discern the inherent contradictions and, in so doing, unwittingly deny Scripture. They interpret biblical categories into psychological ones, thinking the revision will make the Bible more effective in helping people with problems. In the past, struggling Christians clung only to the Bible, but now have "discovered" truth completes revealed truth. So-called behavioral science has now finally come to the rescue of Christians trying to be more like Jesus. Jim Owens writes, "Once we were told we could do nothing without Christ. Now we almost hear that Christ can do nothing in us or for us without the help of 'Christian' psychology. Even the Holy Spirit is pictured as ineffectual without the right counseling methods."[94]

Is the Bible enough? There is no more urgent question at this present time. Is the Bible really enough to help adults and children who are experiencing difficulties in life? Is it enough to help people who are labeled with Attention Deficit Hyperactive Disorder, Oppositional Defiant Disorder, and other "illnesses?" The answer to that question in the minds of many evangelicals is that the Bible is enough for their preaching and/or teaching ministry, but not enough for their counseling ministry. The Bible is inerrant and sufficient for justification, but not enough for putting off sin and putting on righteousness (sanctification). These believers are very orthodox when it comes to upholding the Bible and its message of salvation through faith in Jesus Christ. However, during the rest of the week these believers depend upon medication to relieve anxiety, depression, calm their irrational fears or to help them focus. They rely upon a smorgasbord of self-help, twelve-step, and recovery classes that meet to aid them in their struggles with life. Many of these programs offer believers advice on everything from drunkenness to depression. Much of this advice doesn't even come close to being biblical in nature. The teachings are interspersed with an assortment of contradictory ideas and "insights" of psychology. It is as if the Church today is void of any clear cut theology regarding the nature of man, his problems, and the solutions to those problems.

The issue at stake is the Christian interpretation of life. Is the Bible sufficient to interpret behaviors such as Attention Deficit Hyperactive Disorder, Obsessive Compulsive Disorder, drunkenness or low self-esteem? Can a Christian, using only the Bible, change his behavior so that he pleases God and is socially acceptable? The answer is yes. The Scripture claims to be a sufficient resource for meeting all the difficulties in life, whether emotional or spiritual. The Bible must never be viewed as dependent upon psychology in any part. Jesus is the Wonderful Counselor. Jesus' counseling is never contingent in any way upon the "findings" of ancient or modern psychology. For 1900 years the church has never been at a loss to know how to counsel its members. It was not until the advent of modern psychology that Christians were hoodwinked into believing the Scriptures were incomplete, and for centuries naively counseled people using only God's Word.

---

[94] Jim Owen, *Christian Psychology's War On God's Word.* (Stanley, SC: Timeless Texts, 2003), pp.7-8.

Calling Sin Sickness

Teaching that problems of living can be treated successfully using so-called "Christian" psychology sets aside the historical-grammatical method of interpreting Scripture and replaces it with a hermeneutic centered on pathology. This interpretation views man as a victim, who is sick rather than a sinner. When believers describe sin in terms of sickness (ADHD) the message of the gospel is compromised and undermined. When sin is called sickness the need for repentance is eliminated. There is no need for a Savior. In the same way, when sin is called sickness, sanctification is hindered in the life of the believer. Believers are tricked into thinking they are sick and need recovery. A fornicator may be called to repentance, but if he is sick (he has a "sexual addiction") then he is no sinner. A rebellious child may be encouraged to repent, but if he is sick (ADHD, etc.) then he is no sinner.

We Have Everything We Need

The ominous spread of psychology into the Church is the reason evangelicalism counts for so little in the modern world. It is because believers are failing as Christian people in their daily lives that so few are attracted to God through Jesus Christ. Immorality, rebelliousness to authority, and lack of self-control are as common among Christians as they are the lost. The church is weighted down with iniquity (Isaiah 1:4). Everyone is having troubles. There are large numbers of Christians, who are unhappy, despairing, depressed, and have lost hope for one reason or another. This disquiet, this lack of ease, this tension, and this troubled state has believers looking for answers. Unfortunately, having accepted psychology's diagnosis of man's problems, Christians have eagerly begun to practice psychology's "cure." Church attendance, conversions, and sanctification have declined significantly. The patient is dying on the table and they keep giving him the same "Christian" psychology that made him ill in the first place. Pastors, instead of feeding their sheep the "unleavened bread of sincerity and truth" (1 Corinthians 5:8), are steadily starving their sheep with the leaven of psychology.

The psychological way of ministry has filled the church with a mistaken sense of optimism. Unfortunately, what has been labeled "Christian psychology" is nothing more than the theories and techniques of Freud, Rogers, Jung, Fromm, Maslow and others sandwiched in between a couple of prayers. Imagine atheists and agnostics "empowering" believers for kingdom growth. Jim Owen writes, "It has become my firm conviction that 'Christian' psychology represents one of the most dangerous challenges to the sufficiency and authority of Christ and His Word that the church has faced this century."[95] It is impertinent and arrogant for man to think that he can supplement the Bible with his own ideas. The Bible was given to the Church for the pursuit of her work in salvation and sanctification. The presuppositions of counseling and the methodology must come from the Scriptures. But is it possible for a secular counselor to stumble over some truth that is not contradictory to the Scriptures? May Christians integrate that into their counseling theory and/or practice? After all, "all truth is God's truth." But the truth will be found in a purer form in the Bible, if it is indeed necessary to counseling.

Everything that claims to be God's truth must conform to Jesus Christ who is Truth. All of God's truth is *wholly* true. Error that is mixed with truth contaminates the truth making it error. The devil quoted the Scriptures, but then added his own words. The Pharisees, who possessed considerable knowledge of the Scriptures, "invalidated the Word of God" by mixing it with their traditions (Matthew 15:1-7). What they believed and taught was no longer truth even though it was mixed with truth. "All Truth" must mean that no portion of truth may be mixed with anything else. Jay Adams writes:

> All Truth is Truth. Whatever Truth is revealed in General Revelation must therefore be true, not partially so, or even mostly so. To say otherwise is to say that, in nature, God gave us contaminated truth, or no truth at all. Neither can be correct. Revelation from God is always wholly true. But what truth is revealed through General Revelation? Is it truth about automobile mechanics? About medicine (think of the change in that field!)? About cooking? Or biology or— you name it! Why should psychology be any different? Indeed, there is no proof that psychology—in any of its parts— has been revealed.

> And if it were true that General Revelation may be found in psychology, we must ask *what* psychology?

---

[95] *Ibid.*, p.20.

...there are more than 250 differing psychological systems abroad in this country alone, each competing for recognition as the true one.[96]

Trying to integrate psychology and theology is like a buffet at a restaurant. The buffet contains a wide variety of meat, fish, vegetables, breads, and desserts. A group of believers go through the buffet and when they return to their table they see that everyone has a different combination of food on their plate. In the same way a group of Christians go through a buffet containing several hundred conflicting theories and models of psychology. Each person is looking for "truth." After going through the buffet, they see that they all have different "truths" on their counseling plate. When subjectivism rules, everybody ends up with something different on their plate.

Everything God has revealed in His Word is true. God's Word is inerrant. An integrationist (one who mixes Christian theology with one of the many secular counseling models) may say he has discovered "God's Truth," but how does he establish it as God's Truth? Sin has affected man's thinking and his capability to grasp truth.[97] His thinking has become "darkened" and though he professes to be wise, he is "foolish" (Romans 1). For that reason, psychologists are constantly discarding their theories for new ones. The theories integrated into "Christian" psychology and called "truth" by "Christian" psychologists are no longer true.

God's Word teaches that all Christians posses everything they need for real victory and change. When our Lord completed His redemptive work He omitted nothing. Those who have been saved are granted everything pertaining to life and godliness. The Apostle Peter wrote, "Seeing that His divine power has granted to us everything pertaining to life [salvation] and godliness [sanctification], through the true knowledge of Him [not the strange doctrines of Freud and Rogers] who called us by His own glory and excellence" (2 Peter 1:3, italic and brackets ours). Believers are complete in Christ Jesus (Colossians 2:10).

---

[96] Jay Adams, *Is All Truth God's Truth?* (Stanley, N.C.: Timeless Texts, 2003), pp. 7-8.

[97] Man is biased and limited in his ability to grasp truth. Nevertheless, God's Truth can be known. The Holy Spirit moved on the prophets and apostles to write Truth. Likewise, the Holy Spirit enables a man to correctly interpret and use the Bible. That is why Jesus called the Holy Spirit the Spirit of Truth (John 14:17). The emphasis is that the Holy Spirit always works in conjunction with God's Word, not Freud's, Rogers', Maslow's, etc.

Our sufficiency is not in ourselves and certainly not in any man. The Apostle Paul wrote, "Not that we are sufficient of ourselves to think any thing as of ourselves; but our sufficiency is of God" (2 Corinthians 3:5 KJV). Expanding on this great truth, he further stated, "And God is able to make all grace abound to you, that always having *all* sufficiency in *everything*, you may have an abundance for every good deed" (2 Corinthians 9:8, italics ours). God has provided all the necessary resources we need to meet the challenges of life.

Psalm 19 and 119 are about the sufficiency of Scripture. It is important that every biblical counselor learn to use these psalms in defending their commitment to counseling biblically. As you read them notice these are the same claims made by psychology, thus making psychology competitive with God's Word.

Psalm 19 says that the Scriptures are sufficient. The Scriptures are "perfect, restoring the soul." What more does the Christian need? The Scriptures are *perfect*. They are complete and whole. They do not need to be supplemented by man's theories. How can human wisdom enhance perfection? The Scriptures *restore* the soul. The Scriptures are adequate for changing people's lives. The Scriptures can transform a depressed person into a peaceful and happy person (19:8). The Bible can *enlighten* a person as to the cause and cure of his problem (19:8). And because the Scriptures are perfect and can restore a man's soul, they are more valuable than all the theories, myths, strange doctrines, and speculations of men (19:10).

Psalm 119 is also about the sufficiency of Scripture and is full of help for counselors and their counselees. The psalmist wrote, "Thy testimonies also are my delight; they are my counselors" (119:24, KJV). Hard as it may seem, there are many believers who delight in Carl Rogers' client-centered therapy or Abraham Maslow's hierarchy of needs. They delight in their feelings of significance and worth. As biblical counselors, it is our job to point children or adults labeled ADHD to the Word of God. The psalmist continues, "My soul cleaves to the dust; revive me according to Thy word" (119:25). It is God's Word that will revive and change a person.

Models of counseling that deny the Scriptures altogether or deny the Scriptures by denying the sufficiency of the Scriptures must be hated. The psalmist wrote, "From thy precepts I get understanding [understanding as to why little Archie is fidgety, does not pay attention, complete a task, etc.], therefore I hate every false way. Thy word is a lamp to my feet, and a light to my path" (119:104-105, brackets ours).

Jesus prayed for His disciples, "Sanctify them in the truth; Thy word is truth" (John 17:17). There is no statement in all of Scripture that so clearly declares that sanctification in its fullest sense is accomplished by God's Word. The so-called experts, secular and Christian, insist the Bible is insufficient for sanctification. The fact is that the Scriptures give us more insight into the cause and "cure" of the behaviors labeled ADHD, ODD, etc. than all the experts. The psalmist declares, "I have more insight than all my teachers, for thy testimonies are my meditation" (Psalm 119:99).

God testifies that His Word is wholly adequate for every need. Paul wrote, "All Scripture is inspired by God and profitable for *teaching*, for *reproof*, for *correction*, for *training in righteousness*; that the man of God may be adequate, equipped for every good work" (2 Timothy 3:16-17, italics mine). That the Word of God is sufficient is demonstrated in four ways. God's Word teaches truth, reproves sin and error, corrects behavior, and trains in righteousness. The Scriptures are adequate to show parents what's right, what's wrong, what needs to be done to help their child labeled ADHD and how to help them change.

While an integrationist may truly admire the Bible, his reliance on psychology shows an equal, if not greater, confidence in secular theories and therapies. If he blends Scripture and psychology, then he does not believe the Scriptures are sufficient. If the Scriptures are not sufficient, then Christ is not sufficient. To maintain Christ's sufficiency while at the same time saying Christ's Word is deficient is absurd. Christ and Christ's words are inseparable. It is through the written Word of God that we come to understand the living Word of God.

Counseling has always been part of the normal activity of the Church. God has given pastors and elders the task of teaching and changing people's lives (sanctification) through the authoritative ministry of His Word (2 Timothy 3:15-17). Pastors often claim they do not have time to counsel individuals. Counseling was a major part of Paul's ministry. Paul wrote, "And we proclaim Him, admonishing *every man* and teaching *every man* with all wisdom, that we may present *every man* complete in Christ (Colossians 1:28-29, italics ours). Notice that Paul said "every man." In Acts, Paul is quoted as saying, "Therefore be on the alert, remembering that night and day for a period of three years I did not cease to *admonish each one* with tears" (Acts 20:31, italics ours). Paul's ministry of the Word not only included public preaching, but "admonishing" individuals. The word "admonish" is the Greek word *noutheteo*, from which Jay Adams coined the phrase "nouthetic counseling."[98] To admonish or warn an individual is one of the elements of nouthetic or biblical counseling. There is something in the individual's life that God wants to change. Paul says he admonished individuals for their sinful behaviors and attitudes. Luke further recorded Paul's words, "How I did not shrink from declaring to you anything that was profitable, and teaching you *publicly* and from *house to house*" (Acts 20:20, italics ours). Paul ministered the Word publicly and from house to house. Paul visited individuals and families who were having difficulties, just as people do today, and he taught them using the Scriptures. Nouthetic ministry is how the New Testament Church functioned. All believers are commanded to "admonish one another" (Romans 15:14); "encourage one another" (Hebrews 3:13); "comfort one another, and build up on another" (1 Thessalonians 5:11); and if a believer is caught in a sin, we are to "restore one another" (Galatians 6:1). To help one another, by skillfully using and applying God's Word, is the duty of all believers.

After Charles Darwin's theory of the random universe, the second greatest challenge to Christianity in the last century came from Sigmund Freud. Psychoanalysis and all the other theories and models of psychology have been a major force in secularizing society and the Church. Freud was very aggressive and always on the attack against Christianity. Freud believed, if science was to flourish, the credibility of Christianity must be destroyed. But modern psychology did not destroy Christianity in the sense that it wanted to. However, by the mid-1970s psychology was well on its way to becoming totally integrated with Christianity. The greatest source of growth in the field of psychology has come in "Christian" counseling which mixes techniques from secular psychology and theology.

Biblical counseling has been replaced by "Christian psychology." This influential movement, which is a form of Gnosticism, gleans its techniques and wisdom from secular humanistic and biological psychology. "Christian" psychologists, who blend theological ideas with ideas from Freud, Rogers, or Jung, often sound vaguely biblical. These extra-biblical theories have opened a flood gate to a variety of church programs based on the presupposition that God's Word is

---

[98] For a further study in the presuppositions and practices of nouthetic counseling, see Jay Adams books *Competent to Counsel, The Christian Counselor's Manual*, and a *Theology of Christian Counseling*, published by Zondervan Publishing House.

incomplete and insufficient. In order to successfully live the Christian life, Christians have become conditioned to turning to human expertise in the field of psychology. They have bought into the lie that the Scriptures are lacking, deficient, and unable to help people who are experiencing deep emotional problems. Christians are convinced that real help lies in adapting secular methods which explains the endless proliferation of twelve-step recovery programs in churches today. Believers have turned away from their pastors and fellow believers and have gone to the psychological clinics. All this has lessened the Church's confidence in the Bible, prayer, fellowship, and preaching as a means through which the Holy Spirit of God works to change people's lives.

In contrast, there is another movement in the Church. Christians are asking what is wrong and what can be done about it. They discern that the condition in which the Church finds herself is mainly due to the departure of men and women from the Word of God. They see that the Church has lost sight of the sufficiency of Scripture, is under the influence of psychology, and that Christianity has turned into nothing more than an approved form of humanism. In other words, the wisdom of man has replaced the sufficiency of divine revelation.

The Bible is *the* counseling textbook. Biblical counseling is grounded in the conviction that God has spoken to and about human beings. The Bible gives the counselor the right *presuppositions* he needs to counsel. Presuppositions have to do with what the counselor is to believe about God and man. The Bible gives the counselor the *methodology* he is to use to minister to his counselee. This has to do with the process of counseling. The Bible gives the counselor the *content* of counseling. What exactly does the counselor say to the counselee? What will I say to an adult or child who has been labeled ADHD?

About the Authors

David M. Tyler, a native of Illinois, has served as a pastor in Southern Baptist churches in Illinois and South Carolina. He holds a B.A. in Theology, an M.A. in Pastoral Ministry, and a Ph.D. in Biblical Counseling. Presently, Dr. Tyler is the Director of Gateway Biblical Counseling and Training Center, in Fairview Heights, Illinois. He is certified by the National Association of Nouthetic Counselors and the International Association of Biblical Counselors. Dr. Tyler is the Vice President of the Board of Directors of Master's International School of Divinity in Evansville, Indiana. He serves on the board of directors of Personal Freedom Outreach in St. Louis, Missouri. Dr. Tyler also lectures and leads workshops on Biblical Counseling. He is the author of *Jesus Christ Self-Denial or Self-Esteem, Self –Esteem: Are We Really Better Than We Think?*, and co-author of *Deceptive Diagnosis: When Sin Is Called Sickness.*

Kurt P. Grady is associate pastor and director of Cornerstone Biblical Counseling and Learning Center at First Southern Baptist Church in Cahokia, Illinois. He earned both Bachelor of Pharmacy and Doctor of Pharmacy degrees from the St. Louis College of Pharmacy and completed residency training at the University of Florida Health Science Center in Jacksonville emphasizing adult critical care. He subsequently earned a Masters degree in Business Administration from Southern Illinois University at Edwardsville. Dr. Grady holds a Doctor of Biblical Studies degree with an emphasis in Biblical Counseling from Master's International School of Divinity in Evansville, Indiana and he is currently pursuing Master's of Divinity degree from the same institution. His ongoing research interests are in the areas of unnecessary psychiatric drug therapy and the impact these drugs have on a Christian's progressive sanctification. Kurt is certified by the International Association of Biblical Counselors and he is a member of the Christian Pharmacists Fellowship International. With Dr. David Tyler, he is the co-author of *Deceptive Diagnosis: When Sin Is Called Sickness* by Focus Publishing. Kurt has published several articles and he lectures and leads workshops on biblical counseling topics.

Also by David Tyler & Kurt Grady:

Deceptive Diagnosis:
When Sin is Called Sickness

To order contact:
www.focuspublishing.com